Food Allergy Relief

ABOUT THE AUTHOR

James Braly, M.D., is best known as a world authority on food allergy. He introduced licensed laboratory food allergy assays to U.S. physicians in the 1980s. By means of a popular professional newsletter, he helped to disseminate the international scientific literature about delayed food allergy and food subfraction sensitization to American health professionals. He recently was involved in the introduction of new ELISA assays for the screening of celiac disease. Dr. Braly also has been one of the leading clinicians in the identification of etiologies and natural therapies for food allergies.

Today, Dr. Braly is senior medical editor of the monthly E-mail newsletter "Food Allergy & Nutrition Update" and a monthly newsletter for independent pharmacists, "The Herbal Pharm." He currently is working on his next full-length book.

In addition, Dr. Braly is involved in teaching, lecturing, and consulting, as well as product research and development. For information about his services, phone (954) 927-2850; fax (954) 927-2332; e-mail info@drbralyallergyrelief.com; or visit the Web site at www.drbralyallergyrelief.com.

Food Allergy Relief

JAMES BRALY, M.D.
WITH JIM THOMPSON

K

KEATS PUBLISHING

LOS ANGELES

NTC/Contemporary Publishing Group

Eleanor Kong, Pharm. D.

Library of Congress Cataloging-in-Publication Data

Braly, James.
           Food allergy relief : the joys of being food-allergy free, the natural way /
   James Braly ; Jim Thompson, editor.
               p. cm.
           Includes bibliographical references and index.
           ISBN 0-658-00723-8 (paper)
           1. Food allergy—Popular works. I. Thompson, Jim. II Title.

   RC596. B726 2001
   616.97'5—dc21

                                       00-042422

Managing Director and Publisher: Jack Artenstein
Executive Editor: Peter L. Hoffman
Director of Publishing Services: Rena Copperman
Managing Editor: Jama Carter
Project Editor: Claudia L. McCowan
Text design by Wendy Staroba Loreen

Published by Keats Publishing
A division of NTC/Contemporary Publishing Group, Inc.
4255 West Touhy Avenue, Lincolnwood, Illinois 60646-1975 U.S.A.Printed and bound in the United States of America

International Standard Book Number 0-658-00723-8

00 01 02 03 04 DHD 18 17 16 15 14 13 12 11 10 9 8 7 6 5 4 3 2 1

Contents

Chapter 3
GLUTEN SENSITIVITY AND CELIAC DISEASE   41

Chapter 4
CAUSES OF FOOD ALLERGY   51

ACKNOWLEDGMENTS

I want to thank the following people for their expertise: Dr. John Rebello, Dr. Jeffrey Bland, Dr. Jonathan Brostoff, Dr. J. Egger, Dr. Sidney Baker, and Ron Hoggan. Many thanks to John Kernohan, Chris Moore, and Dane Woodruff for making my love of writing and editing an almost painless reality.

A special thanks to my best friend, Rachel Asher—a blossoming writer in her own right—for her help in making the book a friendlier read; to my brother, Charles, who always manages to be there with his sage advice when I need it most; and to my wonderful son, Zachary, for bringing so much motivation, pleasure, and happiness into my life.

Introduction

Most of us have allergic symptoms to commonly eaten foods, but we don't know it. Those of us who suspect that food allergy is a problem don't know how to recognize which foods we're allergic to. Some of us may figure out which foods are causing problems, but we don't have a clue what brought on our allergies in the first place.

As with most other therapies in contemporary medicine, we end up treating symptoms, not causes of disease. Not treating causes of symptoms prevents us from achieving long-lasting allergy relief, and allergy then becomes a lifelong sentence. Wellness is denied and the food allergy epidemic keeps growing larger and larger. This book is intended to put you back in the driver's seat and help you achieve permanent allergy relief—without the need for medication.

The book begins by instructing you on the important differences between immediate and delayed food allergy, and how delayed food allergy is most often the "monster" lurking within the allergy epidemic. You will learn why food allergy is so difficult to recognize and rarely treated. You will find surprising new research about gluten sensitivity, thought to affect more than 10 percent of all Americans and Canadians. You'll read about a serious form of gluten sensitivity, celiac disease, and its unexpected association with cancer, osteoporosis, and diabetes, and the benefits of early discovery and treatment. One complete chapter is devoted to detecting your hidden food allergies and screening for celiac disease. You'll also learn that exciting advancements in laboratory diagnosis and detection today can provide you with accurate tools not available to allergy sufferers a decade ago.

Finally, this book focuses on the major causes of food allergy. You will discover that most of these causes involve bad or misguided choices that you make every day. This means that most of the causes of your food allergies are identifiable, avoidable, and reversible. The sections on causes of food allergy and natural, cause-oriented therapies for food allergy are my favorite and the most optimistic part of the book. I hope you will agree.

What Is
a Food
Allergy?

FOOD POISONING IS NOT A FOOD ALLERGY

The problem of food poisoning is substantial and can happen in several ways. Some naturally occurring plants and animal life are simply unsafe for human consumption; examples include the death cap family of mushrooms, some species of blowfish, and foxglove. More commonly, food poisoning results from spoiled or improperly cooked food. Bacteria with obscure names such as *salmonella, listeria, enterococci,* and *E. coli* can contaminate chicken, beef, and other foods. Each year, contaminated foods result in 5,000 deaths, 325,000 hospitalizations, and more than 76 million cases of digestive illnesses.

Food Additive Sensitivity Is Not A Food Allergy

A discussion of food allergy would not be complete without a brief mention of chemical food additives. All important studies of delayed-onset food allergy have concluded that food additive sensitivities are common and always accompany food allergy. Here are four prevalent food additives associated with chemical sensitivities in food-allergic patients:

1. MSG (monosodium glutamate), a common taste enhancer found in Chinese food, much of restaurant fast food, and many canned, packaged foods.
2. Sulfites/metasulfites/metabisulfites, used to maintain freshness, commonly found in factory-prepared foods, white wines, often added to potatoes, avocados in guacamole dip, shellfish, greens, and vegetables in restaurant salad bars. Asthmatics may have severe reactions to sulfites. Sulfite sensitivity may be associated with a molybdenum trace mineral deficiency.
3. Tartrazine (FD&C yellow #5), used widely as a food coloring, a known cause of hyperactivity, migraines, and asthmatic attacks, depletes body of pyridoxine (vitamin B_6).
4. BHA and BHT, common stabilizers to oxygen.

One aspect of reactions to food additives is the so-called "pseudo-allergic" reaction. An example is hives or urticaria (eruptions of welts or itchy bumps on skin). In children with chronic hives (as opposed to acute, one-time-only eruptions), one must immediately think of food additives (food colorings, preservatives, emulsifiers, taste enhancers, and so on). In a recent double-blind, placebo-controlled study, three out of every four children with chronic hives greatly improved within two weeks on a food additive–free diet. Half the children had experienced complete remission of hives six months later, and lasting improvement occurred in all but one child.

Reactions to foods, even in proven food-allergic patients, often involve "pseudo-allergic" reactions to chemical food additives.

FOOD INTOLERANCE IS NOT A FOOD ALLERGY

A food intolerance refers to a nonimmunological response; that is, a symptomatic response where no observable or measurable immune reaction can be found. The most universal example of food intolerance is cow's milk lactose intolerance. A person intolerant to milk sugar, or *lactose*, lacks an adequate supply of the lactase enzyme needed to digest the milk sugar. Unfortunately, there is evidence that the majority of milk sugar–intolerant/lactase-deficient individuals simultaneously suffer from cow's milk allergy.

FOOD ALLERGY AND THE IMMUNE SYSTEM

A food allergy develops when your immune system, by means of an odd mixture of immune cells, antibodies, and chemical mediators, reacts in an attempt to reject a food in your diet. Food allergy can result in death—from intestinal lymphomas, osteoporotic hip fractures, and asthma—or can create a living hell with years of unending pain and misery.

There are four different types of immune reactions in food allergy. These are called Types 1, 2, 3, and 4. More than one type of reaction can occur at the same time in the same allergic individual.[1] Types 1 and 3 will be the foci of this section.

Type 1 Immediate-Onset Food Allergies

The best known and well-studied form of food allergies is called a Type 1 immune reaction. Type 1 food allergies occur in less than 5 percent of the population, and mostly in children. They also are called immediate-onset, IgE-mediated, and/or atopic food allergies.

Usually occurring in the genetically predisposed individual, the immune system begins creating a specific type of antibody called *IgE (immunoglobulin E)* to certain foods. One side of the IgE antibody will recognize and tenaciously bind to the allergic food. Before this happens, however, the other side of the IgE antibody must become attached to a troublesome, unstable immune cell called the *mast cell*. Mast cells are found almost everywhere in the human body, but are especially concentrated in the lining of your digestive tract.[2] Primed for action, the IgE-coated mast cells now only have to patiently wait for reexposure to food allergens. When you eat the allergy-causing food the next time, IgE antibodies on the surface of mast cells hungrily latch onto the food. Instantly, histamine and other allergy-related chemicals, called *chemical mediators,* come gushing out of the mast cells, rapidly causing the unwelcome symptoms of stomach cramping, diarrhea, skin rashes, hives, swelling, wheezing, or the most dreaded of Type 1 reactions, *anaphylaxis.*

More About Immediate Allergic Symptoms

The symptoms of immediate food allergies first appear just like their name implies—quickly, from a few minutes to two hours after the food is eaten. The most common target areas of immediate-onset food allergy involve the skin, airways, and intestines. Skin reactions such as rashes, hives, or eczema may occur. Intestinal symptoms include vomiting, nausea, stomach cramps, or dull aching, bloating, heartburn, indigestion, constipation, gas, and/or diarrhea. Other immediate symptoms include the coughing and wheezing of asthma or the sneezing, stuffy nose of a patient with allergic rhinitis.

How often and how severe the immediate food reactions become varies greatly from person to person. At the extreme end of the scale, anaphylaxis may occur. Anaphylaxis is a potentially life-threatening Type 1 reaction that can cause suffocation and death from the rapid swelling of the tongue and throat. It also can result in hives, a rapid drop in blood pressure, heartbeat irregularities, and loss of consciousness.

Mast Cells, Histamine, and Immediate-Onset Allergies

In Type 1 allergies, the immune system must first become sensitized to the food. It does this by producing lots of IgE antibodies. Once these food-specific antibodies have been manufactured, but before they can prey on allergic foods, they must first migrate and attach to the surface of a very unique group of immune cells called *mast cells.* Mast cells are specialized, multifunctional immune cells found in the linings of the digestive tract, airways, urinary tract, and skin. They surround small blood vessels (capillaries) wherever they are found—which is just about everywhere.

When functioning properly, mast cells are beneficial, possessing antibacterial and antiparasitic functions.[3] When unstable and coated with IgE antibodies, however, mast cells can cause allergic symptoms.

Once coated with food-specific IgE antibodies, the mast cell pump is now primed for allergy. When a person eats the food again, the IgE antibodies latch on tightly to the food allergen, causing the mast cells to suddenly "degranulate," and release a truckload of histamine and other chemical mediators into the surrounding tissues and bloodstream. The result is abnormal leaking of the gut lining and walls of blood vessels, swelling, pain, cramping, itching, sneezing, mucus, and wheezing. It is these chemicals released from mast cells that cause many of the symptoms and illnesses associated with Type 1 immediate food allergies.

Here's a partial list of diseases where food allergy and mast cell degranulation may play important roles:

- allergic dermatitis, eczema
- psoriasis
- rheumatoid arthritis
- interstitial cystitis[4]
- epilepsy
- nonseasonal allergic rhinitis
- ulcerative colitis
- Crohn's disease

Fortunately, therapy for food allergy includes a variety of antiallergy prescription drugs and phytochemical/herbal extracts that are able to stabilize mast cells, cut back on the excessive release of histamine, and reduce the symptoms of allergy (see chapter 6, pages 78–80).

Type 3 Delayed-Onset Food Allergy

Although less well studied, Type 3 immune reactions are much more commonly involved in food allergy than Type 1 reactions.

A Type 3 food allergy also involves the immune system. Type 3 reactions occur when your immune system creates an over-abundance of IgG antibodies to a particular food. The IgG antibodies, instead of attaching to mast cells like IgE antibodies in Type 1 allergies, bind directly to the food as it enters the bloodstream, forming different sizes of circulating immune complexes. The allergic symptoms in Type 3 immune reactions are delayed in onset, appearing two hours to several days after consuming allergic foods (migraine headaches characteristically first appear forty-eight hours after allergic foods are eaten).

Delayed reactions may emanate from any organ or tissue in the human body, provoking more than one hundred allergic symptoms and well over one hundred medical diseases.

Below is a partial list of illnesses that may be caused or aggravated by IgG-mediated delayed food allergy (many of these conditions will be discussed later in more detail):

- allergic rhinitis, nonseasonal
- ankylosing spondylitis
- anxiety, panic attacks
- asthma
- attention deficit hyperactivity disorder (ADHD)
- autism (due to milk and gluten cereals)
- bed-wetting
- depression
- diabetes, insulin-dependent
- eczema
- epilepsy (with history of migraines or hyperactivity)
- fatigue, chronic
- fibromyalgia
- headaches (migraine, cluster)

- inflammatory bowel disease (cow's milk enterocolitis, Crohn's disease, ulcerative colitis, and celiac disease)
- iron deficiency anemia
- irritable bowel syndrome
- middle ear disease (acute otitis media, serous otitis media)
- rheumatoid arthritis
- sleep disorders (insomnia, sleep apnea, snoring)

No one knows exactly how many people in the United States suffer from food allergies, but the number may run into the tens of millions. Only 5 percent of children under six years old and 2 percent of adults have Type 1 immediate-onset food allergies. Type 1 food allergy is rare and is usually self-diagnosed. Type 3 is very common, seldom diagnosed, and poorly treated.[5] It is Type 3 delayed-onset, IgG-mediated food allergies that are the primary focus of this book.

IMMEDIATE VERSUS DELAYED-ONSET FOOD ALLERGY

Remember the scene in *Mrs. Doubtfire* where Robin Williams, out of blind jealousy, almost killed his ex-wife's allergic suitor with cayenne pepper? That was an extreme example of Type 1 immediate food allergy. This type of immune reaction happens when allergic symptoms to a food occur quickly, right after consumption of a small amount of an allergic food, and the cause-and-effect relationship between the food and the symptoms is obvious.

However, there is the much more prevalent, far more subtle, and insidious Type 3 delayed food allergy that demands our attention. Here's an overview of the important differences between these two types of food allergies:

- Immediate food allergy, once thought to be the only "true" food allergy, is common in children, but rare in adults.
- Delayed food allergy, once thought to be uncommon, now is thought by many investigators to be the most common form of food allergy in children and adults.
- Allergic symptoms in immediate reactions occur within two hours of eating.
- Allergic symptoms in delayed reactions do not appear for at least two hours, not infrequently showing up twenty-four to forty-eight hours later (there are even reports of delayed symptoms appearing three to seven days after eating).
- Immediate-onset food allergy involves one or two foods in the diet, as a rule.
- Delayed reactions characteristically involve three to ten foods, and sometimes as many as twenty foods in very allergic, "leaky" individuals.

Because a small amount of a single food is involved and the allergic symptoms appear quickly, immediate food allergy is usually self-diagnosed: You eat the food; it causes symptoms; you see the connection; you avoid that food. Due to a combination of delayed symptoms, multiple foods, and food cravings, Type 3 delayed-onset food allergies are rarely self-diagnosed. To detect the allergic foods here you will need the skills of a health professional who's knowledgeable about food allergies and about the laboratory immunoassays needed to help discover your particular allergy foods.

- Immediate food allergy involves foods that are rarely eaten.
- Delayed food allergy involves commonly eaten foods—foods you eat every day and may even crave.
- When people quit eating the foods that cause immediate allergy symptoms, they have no withdrawal or detoxification symptoms. They don't crave or miss these foods.
- Powerful addictive cravings and disabling withdrawal symptoms are reported in more than 30 percent of delayed food allergy patients when they stop eating offending foods.
- Immediate reactions to foods primarily affect the skin, the airways, and the digestive tract.
- Virtually any tissue, organ, or system of the body can be affected by delayed food allergy. This includes the brain, joints, muscles, hormone-producing glands, lungs, kidneys, and nervous system. In fact, delayed-onset food allergy is linked to more than one hundred medical conditions involving every single part of the body and some hundred different allergic symptoms.
- Immediate-onset food allergy is often a skin-test positive allergy. The doctor can diagnose it with a simple skin test.
- Delayed food allergies are skin-test negative. The traditional skin tests are poor tests for detecting delayed food allergies. Instead, delayed reactions to food often require state-of-the-art blood tests. These tests detect serum levels of IgG antibodies to foods—IgA as well as IgG in gluten sensitivity and celiac disease (see chapter 5).

- Immediate-onset food allergies are frequently permanent and fixed allergies. For example, once you develop an allergy to peanuts or shellfish, it's for life.
- Delayed-onset food allergies are commonly reversible. If you strictly eliminate the allergic foods for three to six months, you can bring most of them back into your diet and remain symptom-free.

Because delayed-onset food allergies so often are undetected and untreated, they lie behind many chronic medical conditions of unknown cause. These chronically ill people suffer for years, even decades, without ever suspecting that their health problems are rooted in what they eat (chronic pain syndromes such as rheumatoid arthritis and migraine headaches come to mind). When they finally identify and eliminate allergic foods, accompanied by a four-day rotation diet (see chapter 6, pages 71–76), they get quick, long-lasting relief.

COW'S MILK: THE MOST COMMON FOOD ALLERGEN?

Since childhood, most of us have been taught that milk is one of the major food groups, a critical source of nutrition, and the best source of calcium. Few American children grow up without hearing one or more adults say, "Drink your milk. Milk is good for you!" There seemingly is something so wholesome about it—that is, unless you are one of the people who have an allergy to cow's milk and milk products.

There are two key points to remember about cow's milk. First, it is one of the two most commonly eaten foods in the American diet, and second, cow's milk is *the* most common food allergen (this includes the milk proteins whey and casein), and one of the most common causative agents in human illness.

Cow's milk may be a contributing factor to middle-ear infections (otitis media). Even though this infection is known to be caused by different infectious agents (bacteria), an allergic response can bring on or exacerbate the condition. In addition to limiting iron absorption, an allergic reaction to cow's milk can damage the inside lining of the intestines, causing slow blood leakage and loss of iron found in red blood cells.

Cow's milk allergy also is one of the top two or three food allergens that can contribute to poor sleep, asthma, eczema, migraines, rheumatoid arthritis, hyperactivity, bronchitis, more frequent infections and longer hospital stays for premature infants, nonseasonal allergic rhinitis, bed-wetting, so-called "growing pains," colic, heartburn, indigestion, chronic diarrhea, chronic fatigue, hyperactivity, depression, autism, epilepsy (only in those with concomitant migraines and/or hyperactivity), and perhaps even insulin-dependent diabetes.

If you are allergic to cow's milk, consuming nonfat or low-fat milk products will only make your allergy worse. Nonfat/low-fat milk is the most allergenic of all dairy products; the least allergenic dairy products are those highest in fat, such as butter and cream. If you or your baby is allergic to cow's milk, you don't help matters by changing to goat's milk or sheep's milk; both goat's milk and sheep's milk contain casein, the same highly allergic protein found in cow's milk.

Not all problems related to cow's milk are allergies. A large percentage of people lose the ability to digest milk sugar, or lactose, as they get older. This is because they lack lactase, an intestinal enzyme needed to digest lactose. In many people, lactose intolerance leads to significant diarrhea, bloating, cramping, and excess gas. Between eighteen months and four years after birth, most Asian, Hispanic, African-American, Native American, and Caucasians of southern European descent gradually lose lactase—one of many clues that human beings aren't meant to drink cow's milk, at least beyond early childhood.[6]

Many dairy farmers in the United States and Europe use synthetic growth hormone to increase milk production in their dairy herds. This has resulted in high levels of insulin-like growth factor (IGF-1) in the milk we drink. Excess IGF-1 is suspected to be a contributing cause of breast cancer.

Antibiotics also are given to dairy cattle to increase milk production. High levels of antibiotics frequently are found in milk. Overuse of antibiotics in farm animals is suspected to be a major contributing factor in the development of antibiotic-resistant bacteria that may eventually infect humans.

With the elimination of cow's milk in allergic women, calcium becomes an issue of particular concern. No one who has seen an elderly lady severely bent over from osteoporosis of the spine can take the issue of calcium loss in the bones lightly. Yet, a 1997 study found no connection between teenage consumption of calcium from cow's milk and the risk of bone fractures later on as an adult.

Inarguably the best and simplest way to protect babies from food allergy and malnutrition is to use the milk meant exclusively for humans. Mother's breast milk is far superior to cow's milk or milk-based infant formulas for babies. Breast milk is superior to soy formulas, too: One-third of infants allergic to cow's milk are allergic to soy protein as well! Exclusive breast-feeding for at least the first four to six months of life clearly is the best.

Cow's milk is the most common food allergen, but we must not lose sight of the many other common food allergens in our diets. Gluten cereals, egg white and egg yolk, soy, corn, peanuts, shellfish, citrus fruits, and baker's and brewer's yeast all make the top ten allergen list.

Milk Allergic? What to Do About Calcium

The U.S. government has launched two new campaigns to boost calcium consumption by children and teenagers—they are at the ages when bone builds fastest—but key to increasing calcium consumption is understanding why it's important and what foods have it. There are other important factors that govern the uptake and use of calcium in our body. Growth hormone plays a significant role in maintaining and building bone and tissue. Calcium's claim to fame is building strong bones and teeth, but research suggests calcium's benefit may extend far beyond bones. Consuming calcium-rich foods and calcium supplements can help to lower blood pressure, prevent colon cancer, lower the risk of strokes in women (400 milligrams of calcium-rich foods or calcium supplements per day), and reduce symptoms of premenstrual syndrome.

If it is true that calcium deficiency is a real problem, how much calcium do you really need and where are alternative sources of calcium to be found?

The Institute of Medicine (the medical arm of the National Academy of Sciences) has set 1,000 milligrams a day as an adequate level for most adults. Teenagers need more—1,300 milligrams—because their bones are growing so fast. The amount needed for other ages varies: 500 milligrams a day for toddlers;

800 milligrams for four- to eight-year-olds; and 1,200 milligrams for people over age fifty. Overall, dairy products such as yogurt, milk, and cheddar cheese pack the most calcium.

If they're not allergic or lactose intolerant, a few glasses of milk a day would meet the need for most children and teens. But it would be better to give half and half, which includes important fats needed for tissue and cellular growth, and this will also help reduce the risk or magnitude of an allergic reaction.

Still, there are many good alternatives—calcium-fortified orange juice, for instance, packs as much calcium per glass as milk. But too much juice should not be consumed because of the high concentration of sugar. This will tend to promote gas because the bacteria in your intestines metabolize the sugar and release gas as the by-product. Other sources that have less calcium than dairy foods include dark leafy vegetables and broccoli (allergic people should be eating lots of fresh vegetables anyway), soybeans, and canned salmon. You even may be sneaking in calcium without knowing it: 2 tablespoons of blackstrap molasses has about 270 milligrams, and a handful of almonds has 100 milligrams. Nuts are therefore a good source of calcium and other nutrients.

What to Do If Your Baby Is Milk Allergic

Cow's milk allergy is one of the most common allergies in infants and young children, and is notorious for causing a wide variety of allergic symptoms. Identifying cow's milk allergy (CMA) and removing cow's milk from the diet of an allergic baby may appear easy enough, but deciding what to substitute for cow's milk is not. Currently, there are three popular choices available to pediatricians and family physicians for their CMA patients:

- Goat's or sheep's milk
- Hydrolyzed (partially predigested, hypoallergenic) soy or milk protein formulas
- Lamb meat–based formula

The challenge in all this is that milk-allergic infants may be allergic to other foods and protein formulas, as well. Consider this: Allergic reactions to other foods, especially to soy, wheat, beef, peanut, and citrus fruits, develop in about 50 percent of proven cow's milk–allergic infants.

Goat's or sheep's milk is not a good substitute in cow's milk–allergic babies. One study of twenty-six young children with proven CMA found all the children also were allergic to goat's milk.[7] Their immune systems couldn't distinguish the cow's milk protein, casein, from goat or sheep casein. In spite of this, some physicians continue to incorrectly recommend goat's milk formulas for babies with cow's milk allergy.

When first introduced commercially, soy formulas were the only available substitute for cow's milk. Today, soy protein formulas are widely used as alternatives for babies with proven cow's milk allergy, as well as for high-risk, allergy-prone infants when human breast milk is not available. However, up to one-third of all cow's milk–allergic infants also are allergic to soy protein. Thus, soy products in the diet of a CMA infant or child should only supply a small amount of the daily food, unless it is an extreme condition where only soy helps.

Mothers of the world, don't despair! Exclusive breast-feeding—and if breast-feeding is not an option, feeding with an extensively predigested (hydrolysate) milk whey formula—is associated with lower incidence of food allergies.

To sum up:

1. Cow's milk allergy is very common among infants and young children and causes a wide array of symptoms and disease. If you find that your child is allergic, getting cow's milk out of the diet is easy; finding nonallergic substitutes isn't.

2. There are several alternative formulas for infants and young children who are found to be allergic to cow's milk. Some substitute formulas may prove to be more than adequate, while others may prove to be harmful. Breast-feeding your baby is always the best option. The next best option is to consider extensively predigested, hypoallergenic baby formulas. Goat and sheep caseins cross-react with cow's milk casein. Because of this, many authorities are advising that goat's and sheep's milk *not* be used as a substitute, and I agree.

3. Your choice of substitute formulas in cow's milk–allergic infants and children requires knowledge about the allergenicity of each alternative food source. This requires prior testing, including testing for Type 3 delayed food allergies (see chapter 5, pages 64–67).

Common Medical Conditions and Food Allergy

FOOD ALLERGIES OF INFANCY AND CHILDHOOD

One obvious fact becomes clear in children: Our changing diets and changing nutritional status are resulting in more and more food allergies. A wide range of childhood diseases may have food allergy at their root. These include:

- asthma
- attention deficit hyperactivity disorder (ADHD)
- autism

- bed-wetting
- chronic diarrhea
- eczema
- failure to thrive
- growing pains
- headaches
- insulin-dependent diabetes mellitus (IDDM)
- iron deficiency anemia
- middle ear disease
- nonseasonal allergic rhinitis
- short stature

Middle Ear Disease (Otitis Media)

There are two types of otitis media: *acute otitis media* and *otitis media with effusion* (also called *serous otitis media*). Acute otitis media involves an infection in the middle ear. Otitis media with effusion involves fluid buildup in the middle ear.

Otitis media (middle ear disease): Food allergy may be associated with otitis media. It is known that bacterial infections are the main culprit, but these may be brought on and exacerbated by allergic foods. Since 1980, otitis media has increased 224 percent in children under age two.

ADHD: 5 to 10 percent (two to four million) of our children under age seventeen have been diagnosed.

Eczema: 5 percent of children born in 1946 had eczema; in 1999 that number was 21 percent.

Bed-wetting: 15 to 20 percent of our children under sixteen years old are affected.

Signs and symptoms of acute otitis media include:

- severe and persistent pain in one or both ears
- ear tugging or pulling
- fever up to 104 degrees Farenheit (fever with chills or fever with a headache may be a sign of more serious complications)
- irritability, lethargy
- loss of appetite, nausea, vomiting, and/or diarrhea
- Concurrent signs of allergic rhinitis (frequent sneezing, runny or congested nose, nose rubbing, eye burning) complicate the picture in as many as 80 percent of otitis media victims

The second common form of middle ear disease involves fluid buildup, and is called *otitis media with effusion.* The signs and symptoms are:

- ear discomfort (ear popping, ear pressure, earache, hearing loss; middle ear disease is the most common cause of hearing loss in the United States)
- behavioral, cognitive, and emotional changes (poor sleeping, irritability, underachieving in school—many of these are signs and symptoms of attention deficit disorder [ADD] and ADHD)
- speech and language problems

The bottom line: There is a runaway epidemic of otitis media in the United States. Fifty-three percent of American kids have at least one episode of otitis media in their first year of life, and that number increases to 67 percent by two years of age. The result is more than 25 million visits to a pediatrician or family doctor each year, and more than 45 million, mostly unnecessary, prescriptions for antibiotics.[8] There is even evidence that the routine, repetitive use of antibiotics in treating otitis media increases the recurrence of middle ear disease three- to sixfold.

Much of this epidemic could be avoided simply by avoiding food allergens. Many of these children may be food allergic. The allergic reactions cause swelling and closure of the eustachian tube that drains the middle ear. This may then allow infections that are present to grow because the immune system cannot clear the infection due to the blockage. Identify the allergic foods and stop the child from eating them; the eustachian tube will open and drain, and the infection and/or fluid buildup will disappear. No more monthly visits to the pediatrician's office; no more prescriptions for antibiotics that don't work very well. It's that simple. Every single child suffering from repeated bouts of otitis media should be tested for food allergy as I describe later. If they are found to be allergic, they should be treated.

Asthma

Food allergies often result in diseases of the airways, such as asthma, bronchitis, rhinitis, and sinusitis.[9] The most serious of these is undoubtedly asthma. There are more than 17 million asthma sufferers in this country, 5 million of whom are children. The situation is even worse in other countries. England, for example, reports that one in seven children now has evidence of asthma, compared to one in twenty-five adults.

Even with earlier diagnosis and more hospitalization (in the United States, asthma is now the ninth leading cause of hospitalization and is associated with 2 million visits to the emergency room each year), deaths from asthma have tripled, and the number of new cases diagnosed each year has increased by 160 percent since 1980. The fatality rate is highest in African-American children (four to six times more fatal than in white children) and the elderly. Asthma is so common among children that it has become the leading cause of school absenteeism for youngsters under fifteen years of age.

Asthma is mostly an allergic disease in which allergens stimulate the release of chemical mediators from sensitized immune cells lining the airways. This causes the airway tubes to become superirritated or hyperreactive and to constrict too easily. When the surrounding tissue becomes swollen, persistent gelatin-like mucus begins to plug up the air passages. The result is potentially serious bouts of wheezing and coughing, easily provoked by laughing, exercising, crying, or breathing cold air. Shortness of breath, pressure in the chest, and difficult breathing, or a "tight throat," all are associated with attacks that make asthmatics literally feel like they are slowly suffocating to death. Symptoms may last for a few hours or may go on for weeks. An attack may never get past the wheezing and coughing stage, or the victim may need all of his energy to keep breathing. Even simple tasks like talking or eating are difficult. Fatigue, fear, and loss of confidence are predictable side effects of chronic asthma.

Why is this debilitating disorder becoming more widespread and increasingly dangerous? The declining quality of our diets resulting in multiple nutrient insufficiencies; stressful or inactive lifestyles; increasing exposure to airborne and food allergens; increased incidence of other allergic conditions (otitis, sinusitis, eczema, and a family history of atopic allergies occur more frequently in an asthmatic); chemicals and toxins in our food, air, and water; overuse of aspirin and aspirin substitutes;

and an overdependence on airway-dilating broncho-inhaler drugs: All these have combined to increase these deplorable statistics.

Mainstream medicine has been disappointing when it comes to treating asthma. Until recently, the assumption that dictated therapy was that asthma basically was an airway-narrowing disease. Consequently, the wheezing and coughing have been treated primarily with medication to dilate or enlarge the airways. So-called "inhaled corticosteroids" also have been thrown into the mix.

The problem with the "dilate-the-airway" remedy is twofold. When used excessively (more than a canister and a half per month), broncho-inhalers are associated with a dramatic increase in death. Long-term use of inhaled corticosteroids in children has failed to permanently alter the course of asthma. In addition, corticosteroids slow the vertical growth of the child by about an inch per year.

An overreliance on symptomatic drug therapy ignores the three major underlying causes of asthma—namely, delayed food allergies, airborne allergies, and malnutrition. And if we ignore the cause, we perpetuate the disease.

A better and more lasting approach in treating asthma is to address the causes, not the symptoms; that is, deal with the underlying causes of airway inflammation and hyperirritability and not just the wheezing and coughing. This sensible approach begins with the identification and elimination of airborne and food allergens.

The most common airborne allergens are dust mites, mold, animal dander (dead skin), and cockroach antigen. Wheat (the glutenin subfraction more than the gliadin subfraction), milk, and eggs are very common food allergens. In some cases, food colorings, preservatives, and other chemical food additives can contribute to the disease.

At the same time, you need to take care of the profound malnutrition found in asthmatics. This includes the asthmatic learning to eat five to nine servings of (nonallergic) fruits and vegetables every day. In addition, daily supplementation should include the following:

- magnesium
- omega-3 essential fatty acids (fish oil and flaxseed oil)
- vitamin C
- natural, mixed tocopherols (vitamin E) with selenium
- glutamine
- methylsulfonylmethane (MSM)
- N-acetyl cysteine (to increase lung levels of the antioxidant tripeptide, glutathione)
- B-complex vitamins

There is evidence that certain standardized herbs and herbal extracts may be beneficial in asthma therapy, such as ginkgo biloba, capsaicin (from cayenne pepper), *Typhlora, Boswellia serrata,* and the "mast cell stabilizers" quercetin with vitamin C, *Coleus forskholii,* and *Picrorhiza kurroa.*

Many asthmatics experience wheezing, coughing, and chest tightness during exercise. This is called *exercise-induced asthma* and is often an expression of food allergy symptoms provoked by the stress of exercise. The food allergy is silent until physical stress is brought into the formula. (The connection between exercise and provoked food allergy also is seen with exercise-induced hives and angioedema.)

If exercise-induced asthma is a problem, here are some precautions to take:

- Identify and eliminate all food allergens from your diet.
- Exercise just before eating or do not exercise for at least three hours after eating.
- Take 2,000 to 3,000 milligrams of vitamin C (children under fifteen should take 500 to 1,000 milligrams) and one to two capsules of cayenne pepper or capsaicin thirty minutes to an hour before exercising.

Bed-Wetting (Nocturnal Enuresis)

Tens of thousands of families have to deal with *enuresis* (the medical term for bed-wetting). Laundry is a real burden, and the ever-present odor of urine can become a problem. The expense of buying disposable diaper underpants and medications can be tremendous. Bed-wetters often are reluctant to go to camp, stay over with friends, or do the things other children normally do. All this leads the bed-wetter to feel that she has become a real liability. As a result, bed-wetting causes a poor self-image and lowered self-esteem.

There can be other problems, as well. Attention deficit hyperactivity disorder (ADHD)—commonly a food allergy condition—is more prevalent in bed-wetters. Bed-wetting kids with ADHD suffer from poor attention span, daydreaming, inability to finish their schoolwork, impulsivity, abnormal restlessness, and inability to sit still. Between 15 and 20 percent of American children—more than eight million—suffer from bed-wetting. Five percent of those who suffer from this problem as children still have the problem in adulthood. Taken together, it is clear that bed-wetting is a serious national problem.

A bed-wetter often suffers from delayed-onset food allergy. Allergic reactions involve the irritation of the bladder wall (cystitis) and sleep disorders. When the food allergy problem is solved, the enuretic sleeps more restfully. She wakes up to urinate and the bedsheets remain dry. A dry bed every night is definitely reward enough, but many other positive results are experienced—ADHD, poor school performance, behavior problems, and poor self-esteem change for the better or disappear entirely.

BRAIN ALLERGIES

Even the human brain is not immune to the effects of food allergy and poor nutrition. Consider this: There are more than eighty neurotransmitters identified in brain function, and at any given moment more than 20,000 biochemical reactions are occurring simultaneously. All of this may be disrupted when one is reacting allergically to foods, so you can see that the potential impact of food allergies on our mental and emotional well-being is enormous.

When the brain is the target organ of allergy, the repercussions mirror those diagnosed in the traditional psychiatric and neurological lexicon. These include:

- major depression and dysthymia, or mild, prolonged depression (perhaps the most common presenting symptom of gluten sensitivity, this is associated with lowered concentration of metabolites of three major brain neurotransmitters: serotonin, dopamine, and norepinephrine)
- violent suicide
- impulsive behavior, obsessive-compulsive behavior
- anxiety, nervousness, panic attacks, phobias

- irritability, hostility, quarrelsome behavior, assaultive behavior/acts of violence, criminal behavior
- hyperactivity, ADHD
- autism
- Down's syndrome (up to 40 percent with celiac disease)
- epilepsy with migraines or hyperactivity
- epilepsy with ataxia (Ramsey Hunt syndrome)[10]
- gluten-induced ataxia
- insomnia and other sleep disorders
- stuttering
- mental fatigue, mental lethargy, loss of motivation
- memory loss, difficulty concentrating, "mental fog"
- mental deterioration, intellectual deficits, dementia
- brain atrophy
- poor blood circulation to frontal cortex
- perhaps certain forms of schizophrenia

Food allergen/antibody immune complexes can settle in your brain and/or cause the malabsorption of brain nutrients. The result can be cognitive, emotional, behavioral, or neuro-electrical seizure upset.

During my years as a clinician I saw emotional, behavioral, and mental problems clear up all the time. ADHD patients got better; sleep-disorder patients began sleeping through the night; many patients presenting with complaints other than brain allergies—such as headaches, arthritis, or obesity—reported back to me that they were feeling more alert, or less anxious and depressed, or that their short-term memory was back to normal and the irritability gone. How did all this come about? Simply by eliminating allergic foods.

Here's a true story. After years of psychiatric therapy, a patient came to me because of his bouts of deep depression. He was unable to work and had lost five jobs in as many years. He had tried many prescription medications; most had affected him adversely. At this time he was on a mood-elevating drug that left him feeling listless and nauseated and seemed to interfere with his concentration.

The delayed food allergy IgG blood test I ordered for him revealed that he was highly allergic to both milk and cereal grains—his favorite foods. Furthermore, he was very sensitive to the petrochemicals he encountered in his work as a mechanic. In addition to the elimination of food allergens and a strict rotation diet, we prescribed a regimen of supplements targeted at reversing a leaky gut. We also suggested that he seek a new career that wouldn't overload him with chemical irritants.

After four months of therapy, his words were: "The cloud has lifted." His energy level was better than it had been since he was a teenager. A year and a half later he called to say that he was free of depression without taking prescription drugs, and that his family enjoyed "having me back."

ATTENTION DEFICIT HYPERACTIVITY DISORDER (ADHD)

ADHD is fast becoming a household name. In 1990, 750,000 children were diagnosed with ADHD. Today, that figure is quickly approaching three million. ADHD is considered the most common child psychiatric disorder in the United States—3 to 10 percent of our children under seventeen are thought to have the condition. The ratio of boys to girls with ADHD is between three to one and nine to one, but this may decrease with age. Part of the difference between sexes may be referral bias related to disruptive behavior, since boys have more hyperactive/impulsive symptoms than girls. A third or more of ADHD children will grow up to be ADHD adults, unless the underlying causes are identified and treated.

There is no laboratory or clinical test available yet that definitively diagnoses ADHD. The diagnosis is based on a child or adult manifesting the symptoms of inattention, hyperactivity, and impulsivity to the extent that the symptoms impair that person's ability to function.

Most of the 2.5 million children diagnosed with ADHD take medication under a doctor's prescription, usually the amphetaminelike drug Ritalin (methylphenidate), to help them pay attention, calm down, be less disruptive, and perform better in school.

Delayed food allergy and chemical food additive sensitivities may be responsible for many of the ADHD cases observed. Recently it was shown by EEG mapping that when children with food-induced ADHD eat certain foods, those foods may not only influence clinical symptoms but may alter brain electrical activity as well. Clearly, the brain is a target organ in food allergy.

In a classic study by Dr. Egger and colleagues, ADHD children, all of whom were socially handicapped with severe overactivity and inattention, were placed on a very restrictive hypoallergenic diet for four weeks. Egger then openly challenged the children who did well with artificial food colors, preservatives, and foods. A placebo-controlled, double-blind test followed the identifying of allergic foods.

The results? Eighty-two percent of the children got better on the hypoallergenic diet. One out of four severe ADHD children recovered completely. Even more remarkably, most of the other non-ADHD symptoms improved with the diet, as well.

Take a look at these numbers:

Symptoms	ADHD Children Before Diet Change	On Diet
Antisocial	32	13
Headaches	48	9
Seizures/fits	14	1
Abdominal pain or discomfort	54	8
Chronic rhinitis	33	9
Leg aches ("growing pains")	33	6
Skin rashes	28	9
Mouth ulcers (canker sores)	15	5
Emotional problems (depression, anxiety, irritability, hostility)	7	0

During the subsequent reintroduction, the most common substances that caused problems were tartrazine (FD&C yellow #5) and benzoic acid. However, no child reacted to these two food additives alone. A total of forty-six different foods provoked allergic symptoms. Soy, cow's milk, wheat, grapes, chocolate, and oranges were the most common food allergens. Foods that did not cause symptoms included cabbage, lettuces, cauliflower, celery—and duck eggs.

CHRONIC PAIN SYNDROMES

Migraine Headaches

Listen to this migraine sufferer: "When I had headaches, I only lived half a life. When I had a migraine, everything else was obliterated by the pain—my family, my work, my name.

I was living half my life on another planet, a planet of torture and pain."

Migraine headaches affect 30 million Americans. Female victims outnumber male victims nine to one. Thought to be triggered by the dilation of arteries in the scalp and constriction of arteries in the brain, migraines often are associated with visual disturbances, nausea, vomiting, and sensitivity to light and noise. Such headaches are exhausting, and the sufferer usually has to sleep it off afterward.

Cluster Headaches

A cluster headache is the most severe of all headaches, found three times more often in men than in women. It often comes on during sleep and/or twenty to forty minutes after drinking an alcoholic beverage. The severe pain usually is located behind one eye, described as feeling like "a red-hot poker being driven into the eye socket." The incapacitating pain of cluster headaches can last nonstop for hours or even days, and often occur in batches on a daily basis. The pain can become so severe that 20 percent of the victims seriously consider suicide as an alternative to the pain. Accompanying the severe eye pain are increased tearing in the affected eye; stuffiness in the nose; feeling hot; sweating of the face, neck, and trunk; nausea; vomiting; diarrhea; a drop in blood pressure; and even heart arrhythmias.

Other Types of Chronic Pain

Migraine and cluster headaches are just two kinds of chronic pain; there are many others. Millions of people suffer from arthritis, fibromyalgia, low back pain, abdominal pain, and cramping. Doctors traditionally have used aspirin and a wide assortment of painkillers to treat these conditions, with mixed results. Finding the causes and effective therapies for migraines, cluster headaches, and arthritis has proven difficult. Hormonal imbalances, genetic disposition, chronic tension, and psychosomatic origins have been suggested as causes. Even when doctors are able to provide relief, it can only be temporary because they are treating the symptoms, not the causes. (Hippocrates was the first physician who sought causes to treat disease. He was quoted as saying, "Give me fever and I will conquer all disease." He recognized that fever, like pain, is neither the disease nor its cause—it is the effect.)

Many chronic pain sufferers give up hope of ever living a pain-free life again. But too many chronic pain sufferers and their doctors are overlooking a common cause of pain—Type 3 delayed food allergies.

There are signs of progress, of course, as conventional medicine finally is acknowledging that certain foods and food additives trigger many migraines and are also involved in rheumatoid arthritis and fibromyalgia. This brings the truth a bit closer, but still leaves help much too far away for the millions of allergic pain sufferers.

The first avenue of attack on migraine and cluster headaches is the elimination of food allergens and chemical additives and a four-day rotation diet. The majority of migraine and cluster headaches can be traced to delayed-onset food allergy, and more than 90 percent of migraine sufferers recover when they have a personal or family history of Type 1, IgE-mediated atopic allergy.

The most common allergic villains in migraines are cow's milk, eggs, wheat, oranges, benzoic acid, cheese, rye, tomatoes, and tartrazine (FD&C yellow #5). Typical of IgG-mediated, delayed-onset Type 3 food allergies, the median time for migraine symptoms to appear after eating allergic foods is forty-eight hours. Because symptoms are delayed and multiple offending foods always are involved, the allergic foods rarely are self-diagnosed by migraine sufferers. Unfortunately, skin tests for food allergy are not helpful because migraine headaches are a Type 3 food allergy, not a Type 1.

RHEUMATOID ARTHRITIS (RA)

Rheumatoid arthritis is a chronic inflammatory joint disease that afflicts about three million Americans, mostly women. It destroys joints, but can affect other tissues, including the lungs and heart. RA is so disabling that half the people with the disease must stop working within ten years of diagnosis. My fifteen years of clinical experience tells me that rheumatoid arthritis is frequently caused or provoked by food allergy, and that most younger rheumatoid arthritics—those under the age of seventy—respond dramatically to food allergy elimination, a four-day rotation diet, and naturopathic anti-inflammatory supplementation, as needed.

IRRITABLE BOWEL SYNDROME (IBS)

Irritable bowel syndrome is an extremely common medical condition of the intestinal tract, diagnosed by exclusion of other common causes of similar abdominal symptoms, such as milk lactose intolerance, cow's milk colitis, celiac disease, and inflammatory bowel disease. IBS is so common, in fact, that it afflicts 15 to 20 percent of American adults (40 million to 54 million) at any one time. In fact, 30 percent of English people report symptoms compatible with IBS. Next to the common cold, IBS is the leading cause for missing work, and is the number one gastrointestinal condition seen in clinical practice in the United States.

IBS often first appears in the late teens or early adulthood, and is seen primarily in young or middle-aged adults. Female adults are four times more likely to suffer from IBS than males. Interestingly, individuals with IBS often have a history of excessive antibiotic use (a history shared by food allergy sufferers in general).

Irritable bowel syndrome is characterized as a "motility" disorder with episodic spasms mostly involving the large intestine and rectum, but it may affect the rest of the gastrointestinal tract as well. Although IBS has many symptoms that come and go, the most common characteristic is a crampy, colicky pain or a continuous dull aching in the lower abdomen. The pain or ache is often relieved after passing gas or having a bowel movement. It is most associated with constipation and/or diarrhea.

Since IBS pain may appear as a severe "menstrual pain" or as a chronic stomach pain of unknown cause, many unnecessary hysterectomies and exploratory abdominal surgeries have been performed over the years at great expense, without relief, and with occasional life-threatening complications.

Other physical symptoms seen in IBS sufferers include stomach bloating, burning sensations in the pit of the stomach, nausea, and acid regurgitation. Even urinary symptoms are overrepresented in IBS patients, with loin pain and painful urination particularly common in both men and women (recall that urinary symptoms such as bed-wetting are also symptoms of food allergy).

Mental symptoms are seen in almost all individuals with IBS. A majority of them complain of inner tension, easy fatiguing, muscular tension, anxiety, depression, irritability, and hostility. High levels of anxiety and depression are found significantly more frequently in people with irritable bowel syndrome than in both milk lactose–intolerant individuals and healthy controls.

The psychological findings in individuals with food allergy were very similar to those of IBS. (A clinical pearl: Whenever you hear of an individual with multiple physical, mental, and emotional symptoms, suspect delayed food allergies. You'll be right much more often than not.)

Despite all these symptoms, IBS is not life-threatening. Assuming an overeager surgeon doesn't get his hands on the IBS patient first, the condition rarely requires hospitalization. On the other hand, IBS can be a very frustrating illness for both the patient and the physician because they continue to pursue the conventional high fiber and prescription drug therapies while ignoring the presence of food allergy.

Consider these facts:

- Half of all IBS patients claim their pain worsens after eating food.
- Although skin tests for food allergy are negative (i.e., IBS is not a Type 1 food allergy), many patients are "intolerant" to wheat, corn, dairy, eggs, coffee, tea, and/or citrus fruit, all of which are common food allergens seen in Type 3 delayed reactions.
- IBS patients suffer from a "leaky gut" (see chapter 4, pages 55–57).
- Seventy percent of all IBS patients report relief of symptoms when they exclude certain foods from their diets.

The conclusion: Many irritable bowel syndrome patients suffer from delayed food allergies.

INSULIN-DEPENDENT DIABETES MELLITUS AND DIABETOGENIC FOODS

Diabetes is a chronic disease in which the human body either doesn't produce enough insulin or is unable to properly make use of insulin. *Insulin* is the hormone the body needs to convert sugar, starch, and other sources of foods into cellular energy, and it also stores the unused sugars as fat in adipose tissue.

Diabetes is characterized by high levels of sugar in the blood. There are 17 million diabetics in the United States, and 400,000 of them will die this year from complications associated with diabetes, including cancer, strokes, coronary heart disease, sleep apnea, obesity, high blood pressure, kidney failure, and asthma.

There are two varieties of sugar diabetes: Type 1 and Type 2. *Type 2 diabetes* affects about 90 percent of all diabetics. It usually is first diagnosed in adults—thus the term *adult-onset diabetes.* It is characterized by normal or even elevated levels of the hormone insulin. However, insulin in Type 2 diabetes doesn't work well in regulating blood sugar, and blood sugar is elevated as a result.

Type 1 diabetes is usually detected during childhood and is known as *juvenile diabetes.* It is characterized by a deficiency of insulin in the blood. In order to prevent blood sugar levels from growing dangerously high, daily insulin injections are required for a lifetime—thus the term *insulin-dependent* diabetes mellitus (IDDM).

IDDM affects approximately one million Americans, with 29,000 new cases added to the list each year. It is a very serious disease, especially when poorly controlled, and is the leading cause of blindness, kidney failure, and foot amputations. It is different from Type 2 diabetes, because in IDDM the pancreas, the organ that produces insulin, no longer is able to make enough insulin. IDDM also is among the most common contributing factors in heart attacks and premature death (the average age of an IDDM victim at death is about fifty-six years).

Insulin-dependent diabetes mellitus tends to run in families. It also appears to be associated with—and perhaps is caused by—allergy or hypersensitization to certain commonly eaten foods. These so-called "diabetogenic (diabetes-generating) foods" or "food diabetogens" include gluten cereals, soy, and to a lesser degree, cow's milk.

Once the hypersensitization or allergy to diabetogens is established and then maintained by persistent consumption, silent destruction of insulin-producing cells inexorably proceeds. When approximately 95 percent of insulin-producing cells have been inflamed and destroyed, the official diagnosis of Type 1 diabetes is made. At this stage, IDDM cannot be reversed or cured.

International research indicates that early and long-term avoidance of allergic, diabetogenic foods, combined with a highly varied diet of wholesome and nonallergic foods, can reduce the juvenile diabetic's need for insulin by as much as two-thirds. Even more intriguing, very recent animal studies indicate that IDDM might be prevented with strict avoidance of diabetogenic foods *before* clinical IDDM is apparent—that is, well before 95 percent of the cells have been destroyed.

Summary: Common foods eaten by genetically vulnerable people may trigger or cause beta cell destruction and Type 1 insulin-dependent diabetes. Once the cells have been destroyed, IDDM becomes permanent and irreversible. If treated before beta cell destruction, reversal and prevention may be possible.

Recommended preventive therapy:

- In families prone to IDDM, diabetogenic foods, such as cow's milk, gluten cereals, and soy products, should be avoided by the expectant mother throughout pregnancy and during the first six months of exclusively breast-feeding her baby. Evidence suggests that exclusive breast-feeding at this stage may play a pivotal role in the prevention of IDDM later on.
- All IDDM-prone family members need to eat five to nine servings of fresh salads and vegetables daily. This should begin in early childhood and be practiced indefinitely.
- Supplement the diet daily with niacinamide—the nonflushing form of vitamin B_3—at a daily dose of 250 to 1,000 milligrams a day. Evidence suggests that niacinamide protects insulin-producing beta cells from inflammatory damage and destruction.
- Take 200 to 600 IU of natural, mixed vitamin E daily for the same protective reason.
- Periodically, have blood tests performed to determine the serum level of IgG antibodies to gliadin (from gluten cereals), casein (from cow's, goat's, or sheep's milk), and soy. If IgG antibodies are elevated, IDDM may be developing, inflaming, and slowly destroying beta cells. A strict avoidance diet must be implemented immediately.

Prevention of IDDM is the best hope for the genetically predisposed population. Remember: There is no cure once the insulin-producing cells have been destroyed and clinical IDDM has been diagnosed.

Gluten Sensitivity and Celiac Disease

WHAT EXACTLY IS GLUTEN? GLIADIN?

Inside each grain of the gluten cereals—wheat, rye, barley, oats, spelt, kamut, and triticale—is the potentially toxic protein called *gluten*. Gluten can be further subdivided into subfraction proteins, including *gliadins* and *glutenin*.[11]

Bakers the world over love to work with cereals with high gluten content (Canadian hard wheat is an international favorite for this reason). The higher the gluten content, the more elastic, malleable, expandable, and heat-resistant the dough becomes. This results in lighter, softer, more visually attractive and delicious-tasting breads, bagels, pastas, biscuits, and pastries. So popular have high-gluten products become in the United States and Canada that wheat products represent three of the top six foods in terms of calories consumed by Americans. The other three are dairy products (recall that 20,000 years ago there were no gluten cereals or cow's milk in the human diet).

Gluten cereals can be nourishing foods—unless you happen to be among the 10 to 15 percent of Americans and Canadians who have become sensitized. These 30 million people are subject to declining health and have the potential to become victims of celiac disease, a very serious form of gluten sensitivity.

GLUTEN SENSITIVITY AND CELIAC DISEASE

Approximately 30 million Americans are allergic or hypersensitized to the gluten cereals: wheat, rye, barley, oats, triticale, spelt, and kamut.[12] One million of these Americans will go on to develop a potentially life-threatening, but rarely diagnosed and treated, condition called *celiac disease.*

Celiac disease is a permanent, genetic disease of the small intestine, caused by an allergic toxicity to the gliadin subfraction found in gluten cereals (with the exception of oats). In this illness, the small intestine's lining is unmercifully attacked by gliadin (it doesn't take much gliadin, either—less than half a gram a day can cause the disease). The intestinal lining becomes leaky and loses its ability to absorb nutrients from food. Malabsorption and malnutrition occur, with deficiencies in iron, zinc, calcium, magnesium, potassium, and vitamins B_6, B_{12}, folic acid, A, D, E, and K reported.

There is a strong genetic aspect to celiac disease. Seventy percent of identical twins both get it (175 times more prevalent than in the general population), while the number of siblings and offspring who get the disease exceeds 12 percent (thirty times more prevalent than in the general population).

When I was in medical school some thirty years ago, the prevailing medical wisdom was that celiac disease, or CD, was found in less than one in five thousand Europeans and Americans. "Don't expect to see more than a single case of CD in your medical career," was what I was told.

Due to remarkable advancements in laboratory screening for CD, it turns out that the disease occurs much more frequently than ever imagined. According to a random sampling by the American Red Cross, one in 250 Americans suffers from celiac disease (nineteen out of every twenty of whom go undetected and untreated).

More recent studies appearing in the *Lancet* have reported a prevalence of one in 122 of the Irish, one in 85 of the Finnish, one in 70 of the Italians in Northern Sardinia[13], and one in 18 Algerian Saharawi refugee children. All of these new discoveries have been made possible by a new generation of laboratory tests.

Celiac disease is thought to be such a health threat in Italy that the government is considering mandating that all children, regardless if they are sick or not, must be tested for gliadin sensitivity and celiac disease by six years of age.

I also was taught thirty years ago that a physician should be able to diagnose this rarely seen celiac patient a mile away because the signs and symptoms, mostly emanating from the abdomen, were unmistakable: chronic diarrhea/episodic diarrhea with malnutrition; abdominal cramping; abdominal distention or bloating; foul-smelling, bulky stools (steatorrhea); weight loss or poor weight gain; and short stature. We were to expect to hear complaints of weakness, fatigue, and loss of appetite, as well.

Today, the presenting face of CD has changed. Most CD patients no longer present with abdominal symptoms. Instead, we are seeing patients first presenting with:

- chronic psychological depression (may be the most common presenting symptom of gluten sensitivity)
- excess weight or obesity (more overweight than thin and wasted)
- abnormal elevation of liver enzymes of unknown cause
- permanent teeth that have distinctive horizontal and vertical grooves and chalky whiteness
- chronic nerve disease of unknown cause (ataxia, peripheral neuropathy)
- osteoporosis in women that does not respond to conventional therapies
- intestinal cancers (undetected CD is associated with a thirty- to one-hundred-fold—3,000 to 10,000 percent—increased risk of intestinal lymphomas)[14]
- insulin-dependent diabetes mellitus (IDDM)—because 10 percent or more of IDDM patients have or will develop celiac disease, many diabetic clinics and hospitals are beginning to routinely test all IDDM patients for gluten sensitivity and celiac disease
- thyroid disease (both overactive and underactive)— many thyroid specialty clinics in Europe are beginning to routinely test all autoimmune thyroid-diseased patients for gluten sensitivity and celiac disease
- pregnancies with poor outcomes (spontaneous abortions, premature births, low birth weights, iron deficiency)

The only known effective therapy for celiac disease calls for the complete, lifelong elimination of gluten from the diet. No wheat, rye, barley, or oats in any form are allowed in the diet for the rest of one's life. If strictly followed, dramatic resurgence of health occurs. Diseased intestines heal, deficient nutrients are absorbed again, bones get stronger, and the high risk of intestinal cancer returns to a normal risk within five years on a gluten-free diet.

But first, celiac disease has to be suspected and diagnosed!

The very good news is that there has been a revolution going on in laboratory testing and screening for CD (see chapter 5, pages 67–69). If these new tests are utilized intelligently, often—and soon—by health professionals, better health will be realized for the tens of millions of gluten-sensitive people worldwide.

FOODS THAT CONTAIN GLUTEN

If you are among the 10 percent of Americans with gluten sensitivity—or worse, among the one in 250 with celiac disease—and you are told that you have a genetic disease and must give up all the gluten in your diet forever, be prepared for a shock. You will discover that gluten is found in literally thousands of processed, packaged foods. Just go to your local supermarket and start reading labels if you need proof. You will find wheat in soups, sauces, gravies, sausages, and hundreds of other unsuspected foods. Soon you will realize just how much our modern food production system uses gluten, and what a challenge it is to make your diet truly gluten-free.

You will have to begin by avoiding all bread and pasta products, as well as donuts, pies, and cakes. Biscuits, pancakes, waffles, spaghetti, pizza, bagels, muffins, rolls, and baked goods of any kind will have to go, unless the product is clearly and credibly labeled as "gluten-free." It takes less than half a gram of gluten a day—less than 2 percent of a single ounce—to cause toxic inflammation and cell death in your intestines.

You also will discover that eating in restaurants lies somewhere between a challenge and an impossibility. Even meals that seem gluten-free may contain wheat flour used to thicken a sauce or gravy. Your best bet: Avoid eating in restaurants. But if you must, eat simply. Eat single, whole foods without sauces, coatings, or gravies, such as steamed vegetables, fresh fruits, and simply prepared baked or grilled fish, meats, or chicken. Be sure to ask a lot of questions!

Celiac Disease and Insulin-Dependent Diabetes

Type 1 diabetes (IDDM) sufferers cannot produce enough insulin, the natural hormone that controls the amount of glucose (sugar) in the bloodstream. IDDM occurs when enough insulin-producing cells in the pancreas, called *beta cells,* have been destroyed. More specifically, when 95 percent of beta cells have been wiped out, clinical IDDM is diagnosed. From that point in time forward, the youthful IDDM victims will need daily insulin injections to control blood sugar levels and to stay alive. Without daily injections, premature disease and death is inevitable.

Long before clinical IDDM is diagnosed, however, the lymphocytes from the immune system appear to attack and damage beta cells. This is why IDDM is called an *autoimmune disease.* It is my belief that this attack is provoked by an early and persistent exposure to the diabetogenic foods, such as gliadin from the gluten cereals, soy protein, and casein protein from cow's milk. If this were true, the best intervention would be prevention.

There should be a continuous monitoring of the serum of these children long before the diagnosis of IDDM is made, and before the irreversible destruction of pancreatic insulin-producing cells has occurred. Monitoring can be done with lab tests that detect the presence of IgG antibodies (IgG and IgA both for gliadin) specifically produced against these food diabetogens. If the tests detect abnormal levels of food-specific antibodies, permanent and total elimination of these foods is mandatory. Studies of IDDM-prone animals eating diabetogenic foods indicate that if these foods are completely removed before substantial destruction of beta cells, clinical IDDM can be prevented and the destruction of beta cells stopped. Apparently the lymphocytes then stop killing insulin-producing cells, the cells resume the production of insulin, and the need for future insulin injections has been avoided.

CELIAC DISEASE AND OSTEOPOROSIS

Osteoporosis occurs when there is a decrease in bone density and strength that makes the vertebrae and the small and large bones of the leg, arm, and hip brittle and prone to cracking. Approximately 28 million Americans, 80 percent of them women, suffer from this condition. Many elderly people die shortly after suffering an osteoporotic fracture. (My father died within four months of a hip fracture, and spent that time in great pain.)

Undetected celiac disease may play a pivotal role in osteoporosis, especially in those patients not responding well to conventional estrogen and calcium therapies. If you think just taking calcium supplements is the answer, read on.

Today, 1,500 to 2,000 milligrams of calcium daily is recommended by many doctors as a major component in osteoporosis therapy and prevention. I believe calcium supplementation is overrated. Magnesium, zinc, vitamin K, and vitamin D are four of the many "bone nutrients" that I'm convinced are more critical to bone health and bone density than calcium. Vitamin D levels, for example, are significantly lower in women with broken hips than in other women; half the women with broken hips have measurable vitamin D deficiencies. This is because it is known that vitamin D helps with the uptake of calcium in the intestines. Vitamin D is found mainly in animal foods, so do not skimp when it comes to eating foods such as fish, egg yolks, meats, and fortified milk, if there is no allergy.

Undetected gluten sensitivity—whether or not it has led to celiac disease—is commonly found among pre- and postmenopausal osteoporotic women, and even among children who also suffer from osteoporosis. The same nutrient deficiencies found in osteoporosis—magnesium, vitamin D, and vitamin K—also are seen in people suffering from CD.

When celiac disease is properly diagnosed and the osteoporotic CD patient is placed on a strict gluten-free diet of no wheat, rye, barley, or oats, an average 7.7 percent increase in bone density is seen within twelve months.

An important tool to help solve this debilitating bone disease—at least in the patient not responding well with conventional treatments—may lie in suspecting, detecting, and treating gluten sensitivity.

CELIAC DISEASE AND CANCER

In individuals with celiac disease, the immune system against cancer cells also becomes impaired. This condition is known as *lymphocyte reactivity.* It should be no surprise, then, that there is a significant increased incidence of cancers in biopsy-proven celiac disease. At least eighty-two international studies have been published on the increased incidence of cancer in celiac disease.

Consider this startling observation: The risk of developing T-cell lymphomas, a form of small intestine cancer, is thirty- to one-hundred-fold (3,000 to 10,000 percent) greater in celiac disease patients than in the general population. Small intestinal T-cell lymphoma is the most common malignancy, but there also is an increased frequency of small intestine adenocarcinoma and squamous cell carcinoma of the esophagus. Once the celiac-related cancers have progressed to the point of being diagnosed, the prognosis was generally very poor.

On the other hand, if CD is diagnosed before cancer becomes clinically evident and a gluten-free diet is then strictly followed, the risk of intestinal lymphoma decreases from one-hundred-fold back to near normal in five years. The prevention of cancer is the single most compelling argument for routine and repeated screening or monitoring for celiac disease in the diseases in which CD is hugely overrepresented, which includes all cases of:

- osteoporosis unresponsive to conventional therapies
- insulin-dependent diabetes
- autoimmune thyroid disease
- chronic liver disease of unknown cause
- chronic neurological diseases of unknown cause (especially ataxia and peripheral neuropathy)

- short stature in children
- all first-degree family members of people with CD
- epilepsy associated with hyperactivity, migraines, or calcium deposits in the brain
- pregnancies with poor outcomes

Causes
of Food
Allergy

STONE AGE DIET, MODERN DIET, AND GENETICS

Over the past 20,000 years, people have changed very little—genetically, not at all. The same, however, cannot be said of our diets.

Much of modern human disease is caused when an unchanging genetic makeup (which changes about 0.5 percent every one million years, experts inform me) collides head-on with a radical change in our diets. Take a close look at this fascinating comparison between what our ancestors were eating 20,000 years ago, and our typical diet today:

Stone Age Diet	Today's Diet
0 percent of carbohydrates as cereal grains	75 percent of carbohydrate as grains
Great variety of fruits and vegetables	8 to 10 foods make up 80 percent of daily calories (dairy, wheat, sugars, fried potatoes)
Mother's milk and water most common beverages	Soda, coffee, tea, alcohol, and cow's milk most common beverages (Consider this: In the United States and Great Britain, people are drinking more soda than water! Times have certainly changed.)

OVERCONSUMPTION AND MALNUTRITION

Malnutrition can occur for a variety of reasons, only one of which is not eating enough healthy, nutrient-rich foods. With the poor digestion and poor absorption of nutrients associated with food allergy, many of us become malnourished even when eating what would appear to be a healthy and plentiful diet.

Allergic foods pass through the digestive tract. The digestive tract's natural protective tendency is to try to fend off any substance it perceives as harmful or toxic. By attaching antibodies to the allergen, the digestive tract will try to eliminate the food before it can pass into the bloodstream. The food passes out in the stool partially digested at best, and unabsorbed—and with it goes the nutrients.

In addition, with the intake of food allergens, gut hormone release is inhibited, digestive juices are suboptimally released, foods are poorly digested, and again, valuable nutrients are not absorbed. The end result is a lack of good nutrition (a classic example of overconsumption with malnutrition is seen in undetected celiac disease).

An absolute requirement of optimal nutrition is a diet free of food allergens.

MONOTONOUS DIET

Most food-allergic people eat boring, repetitive diets. One of the reasons food allergies are so common—and getting more common every year—is that people eat a monotonous diet. The same limited number of foods are consumed over and over again. Many of these favorite foods are highly allergenic to humans.

Consider these top nine foods, rated by the number of calories consumed annually, as reported by the U.S. Department of Agriculture:

- whole cow's milk
- 2% cow's milk
- processed American cheese
- white (wheat) bread
- white (wheat) flour
- rolls (wheat)
- refined sugar (which accounts for 15 to 21 percent of all calories)
- cola (more soda pop is consumed than water)
- ground beef

Notice the absence of fruits and vegetables in this list. Notice also that dairy and wheat (gluten) products make up the top six foods. Now recall that allergies to cow's milk and wheat are two of the most commonly reported! By repeatedly eating these foods over and over, day in and day out, it is clear why so many people suffer from chronic food allergies over their entire lifetime.

FRUIT AND VEGETABLE DEFICIENCIES

While Americans eat far too much of the common food allergens, a majority of us do not eat enough fruits and vegetables. The overconsumption of dairy products and gluten cereals—foods that many humans were never meant to eat, according to their genetic makeup—and the underconsumption of fresh fruits and vegetables—foods extraordinarily rich in antiallergy and anti-inflammatory nutrients—are two of the leading causes for the dramatic increase in food allergy today. Studies indicate that as daily vegetable consumption goes up, common food allergy–related illnesses go down, including asthma, chronic bronchitis, peptic ulcers (food allergy is overrepresented in *H. pylori*–induced ulcers), and arthritis. Consider these disturbing statistics:

Percentage Americans Consuming USDA Five Servings a Day Minimum Recommendation for Fruits and Vegetables	
Age (years)	**Percent**
1–10	8.7
11–24	11.7
25–50	15.4
51–64	18.9
65 +	22.0

Let's put it another way:

- Eighty-five percent of all Americans don't meet USDA fruit and vegetable daily recommendations.
- Sixty percent of all Americans don't reach the "five a day" bare minimum for fruits and vegetables combined (many researchers are now advocating nine servings).

Allergy sufferers need to eat five to nine servings of (non-allergic) fresh fruits and vegetables daily!

LEAKY GUT SYNDROME

A common cause and consequence of human illness is abnormal intestinal lining leakiness, better known as the *leaky gut syndrome*. Many authorities feel that a leaky gut is a common underlying cause of food allergy, and here's why.

The mucosal lining of the gut is the first point of contact between foods and the immune system. The intestinal lining alone is estimated to contain more immune cells and produce more antibodies than any other organ in the body. It's hardly surprising, then, that the intestinal lining and its immune system is an absolutely crucial defense against food allergens and infections.

Normally, the inside lining of your small intestine serves as a selective barrier with the outside world, preventing entry into the blood circulation of potentially harmful toxins, microbes, and incompletely digested foods from the gut. At the same time, this lining selectively allows the passage of essential vitamins, minerals, amino acids, very small peptides, essential fatty acids, and other nutrients. It permits digested food protein, carbohydrates, and fats to gain easy entry to the bloodstream.

When this lining begins to break down—or become "leaky"—a food allergy problem and toxic overload begins.

Medical science has identified at least twenty causes of a leaky gut. These nine are the most common:

1. Consumption of allergic foods (food allergy is both a cause and consequence of a leaky gut).
2. Alcohol consumption (wine, beer, and hard liquors).
3. Antibiotic overuse and abuse (for example, overuse in domestic animals to enhance their growth or increase milk production; overuse in the treatment of middle ear disease and sinusitis; use in treating viral infections, such as common cold, flu, viral pneumonia, etc.).
4. Nonsteroidal anti-inflammatory drugs (NSAIDs, such as ibuprofen, Advil, Motrin, Nuprin, Actron, Orudis, Aleve, Bayer, Excedrin).
5. Candidiasis or yeast infection (secondary to alcohol, antibiotics, excess refined sugar intake, birth control pills).
6. Parasitical infestation (e.g., *Giardia*), intestinal bacterial and viral infection.
7. Premature birth and premature exposure to whole foods in infants aged four months or younger.
8. "Friendly" intestinal bacteria deficiency (brought on by overuse of antibiotics, alcohol, refined sugars).
9. Glutamine insufficiency (the primary fuel for the intestinal lining and immune system, depleted during periods of extreme metabolic stress, e.g., burns, injuries, major surgery, radiation therapy, extreme endurance sports, high fever, HIV and AIDS, prolonged fasting, starvation, inflammatory bowel diseases).

Treat and reverse a major cause of food allergy—a leaky gut—and you will be treating and preventing food allergy.

THE NEED FOR FRIENDLY INTESTINAL BACTERIA

Inside the intestines is a carefully balanced world of "friendly" and potentially "unfriendly" bacteria. The friendly, health-promoting strains of bacteria, some 180 in number, are called *probiotics*. They include nine strains of bifidobacteria (the *Bifidobacterium catenulatum* group is the most commonly found, followed by *B. longum, B. breve,* and *B. adolescentis*) and forty-six strains of lactobacilli (among the most common are *Lactobacillus acidophilus, L. casei, L. plantarum, L. rhamnosus,* and *L. fermentum*).

Probiotic bacteria have many scientifically proven benefits, including:

- the prevention and treatment of food allergy (e.g., preventing milk-based allergic reactions, improving infant atopic dermatitis, and treating irritable bowel syndrome[15])
- help in the alleviation of intestinal inflammation
- prevention of abnormal gut leakiness or permeability
- prevention and reversal of diarrhea caused by antibiotics, food allergy, and infections
- suppression of Type 1 IgE antibody production
- promotion of food allergy preventing secretory IgA-food-antigen-specific immune responses in the GI tract
- protection against or reduction in the number of food allergy–provoking candida yeast infections (candidiasis) by decreasing the number of *Candida albicans* in the

digestive tract; decreases the overall severity of mucosal and systemic candidiasis[16]

- oral administration of *Bifidobacterium breve* increases anti-influenza virus IgG antibodies in serum and protects against influenza virus infection; may induce protection against various other viral infections[17]

However, the delicate balance of "friendly" and "unfriendly" bacteria can change. Relative deficiency in probiotic bacteria occurs and disease-causing microbes begin to take over and dominate as a result of early exposure to whole foods in infants, poor diets in children and adults, overuse of antibiotics and other prescription drugs, alcohol consumption, or excessive sugar intake. *Intestinal immune cells* (Th2 cells) and the chemicals they release can change in kind and end up promoting inflammation, increasing gut permeability (leaky gut), and impairing digestion.

As a consequence, probiotic supplements—preferably a live mixture of lactobacillus and bifidobacteria strains—are used to treat and reverse this imbalance. Oral probiotics successfully survive stomach acid and rapidly recolonize the intestine.

Examples where probiotic therapy is becoming increasingly commonplace, even among conventional physicians, include the following:

- immediately following all antibiotic therapy
- subjects with either immediate or delayed-onset food allergy, including atopic eczema, cow's milk– and/or soy-caused intestinal inflammations or enterocolitis
- subjects with intestinal disorders such as Crohn's disease, ulcerative colitis, and irritable bowel syndrome
- food allergy–, antibiotic-, or acute virus–induced diarrhea

Probiotic supplementation appears to be an exceptionally promising therapy for any clinical condition associated with an abnormal balance of gut bacteria, gut inflammation, or abnormal gut barrier leakiness—that is, the intestinal conditions consistently seen in food allergy sufferers.

THE IMPORTANCE OF BREAST-FEEDING

One of the most common causes of food allergy begins very early in life. Once, nearly every mother breast-fed her baby. Mother's milk contains a rich supply of essential nutrients and protective immunity to assist the infant until she has matured and can begin to eat whole foods on her own. As breast-feeding has declined during the past century, the prevalence of childhood allergies has increased dramatically.

The scientific literature for over the last thirty years strongly suggests that exclusive breast-feeding during the first four to six months of life delays for years the appearance of a number of the effects of food allergies such as:

- otitis media (middle ear infection and fluid in the middle ear)
- celiac disease (gluten sensitivity)
- wheezing illnesses, such as asthma and chronic bronchitis[18]
- chronic diarrheal diseases
- autoimmune diseases, including insulin-dependent diabetes

The bottom line: If at all possible, babies should be exclusively breast-fed for six months in order to prevent or delay the appearance of food allergy diseases.

OVEREMPHASIS ON HYGIENE?

Paradoxically, overemphasis on cleanliness and a germ-free environment during infancy and early childhood may be a causative factor leading to food allergies later in life.

According to several recent studies, including one published in the July 31, 1999, issue of the *Lancet,* there is a growing body of scientific evidence that too much emphasis on cleanliness and sterile childhood environments may be associated with as high as a 225 percent increased risk of developing allergies. Other studies have observed that children with the highest incidence of infections during infancy or early childhood—that is, the least hygiene—have the lowest incidence of food and airborne allergies later on.

If subsequent studies bear this out, we may have to reevaluate our obsession with cleanliness and conclude that our kids may be—heaven forbid!—too clean. Exposure to germs early on may bring a degree of protection from childhood and adult food allergies.

CAUSES OF IMMEDIATE FOOD ALLERGIES

A primary reason people have Type 1, IgE-mediated food allergies is hereditary.[19] If both your parents have immediate food reactions, there is a 75 percent chance you will, too; if one parent, a 30 to 40 percent chance.[20] In addition, certain people are not genetically predisposed to tolerate certain foods in their diets—gluten cereals among the Irish, Finnish, Italians, and Sardinians comes to mind.

A persistent imbalance of bacterial flora found in the intestines, with a relative deficiency in "friendly" probiotic bacteria, also seems to play a key role. Too few probiotics cause the intestine's immune system to develop a propensity toward allergy. Excessive exposure to a particular type of food, especially very early in life, also may result in a food allergy predisposition—for example, the unusually high rate of rice allergies among the Japanese or cow's milk allergy among bottle-fed Scandinavians and British.

Diagnosing Food Allergy

TESTING FOR TYPE 1 IMMEDIATE FOOD ALLERGY

Doctors use different kinds of tests to identify this rarer form of food allergy. When using skin testing, the doctor or nurse applies to the skin a dilute solution containing a food extract; the skin on the back or forearm are favorite sites. The skin is then scratched or punctured, allowing the food to penetrate through the skin's surface. A positive reaction indicating an immediate food allergy (and IgE-coated mast cell degranulation) appears as a red bump that looks like a mosquito bite within fifteen to twenty minutes.

Equivalent in diagnostic value to skin tests is a blood test popularly known as the *IgE RAST* (radioallergosorbent test).

This test measures serum levels of food-specific IgE antibodies. A spin-off of the IgE RAST is a test called the *IgE MAST*. It also measures serum levels of IgE antibodies.

Two other tests for Type 1 food allergies are a *histamine release test* (generally speaking, this is not a reliable test for food allergy due to spontaneous histamine release from white blood cells) and a *labial provocation test* (a drop of a suspected food is placed on the lower lip where an allergic reaction produces immediate lip swelling, a runny nose, and redness or hives extending to the chin).

Note: Skin tests, IgE RAST/MAST, and other tests listed above only detect IgE-mediated immediate food allergies. They are without value when used to detect IgG-mediated delayed food allergies.

TESTING FOR TYPE 3 DELAYED FOOD ALLERGY

Suspecting IgG-mediated delayed food allergies as a potential cause of chronic illness is the first step on the road to optimum health. Accurate identification and elimination of food allergens is the crucial second step.

The accurate diagnosis of food allergies always has been a difficult challenge. It should come as no surprise that the diagnosis of delayed-onset food allergy has been fraught with seemingly insurmountable challenges since its symptoms show up so slowly in so many forms, from any part of the body, and to so many different commonly eaten foods. It becomes even more confusing when the allergic food makes you temporarily feel better, not worse (food allergy/food addiction) and when a food may not provoke an allergic reaction every time you eat it.

The food-allergic person's tales of woe about trips from one doctor to another are commonplace (the average number of unsuccessful visits my food-allergic patients made to doctors before coming to my clinics for therapy was six).

"I was skin-tested for food allergy and nothing showed up allergic, only to be told later that skin tests were inaccurate tests for most food allergies," related one patient.

Another patient suffering from delayed food allergy recalled, "Once I was tested and found I was allergic to oranges but not to wheat. The next month I took another test that said I was allergic to wheat but not to oranges. That's when I gave up."

For many decades, a test of choice for diagnosing "true" food allergies has been the skin test (see pages 63–64). The problem all along with both skin testing and the IgE RAST blood test has been that they detect Type 1 allergies—the rare kind. *They don't detect Type 3 food allergies at all.*

It was in 1982, at the Second International Symposium on Food Allergy in Vancouver, British Columbia, that I had the first hint that a new food allergy test for delayed reactions might be right around the corner. Published research was beginning to demonstrate that a fundamental mechanism behind delayed food allergy was the penetration of large molecules of incompletely digested food through a leaky intestinal lining into the bloodstream. As food allergens enter the bloodstream, we were told, IgG antibodies—not IgE—were formed against food allergens. IgG antibodies bind to the allergens, forming food allergen/antibody immune complexes.

Circulating throughout the body, these immune complexes, if not cleared and eliminated by detoxifying immune cells called *macrophages* (Kupffer cells in the liver), penetrate the walls of the small blood vessels, depositing in various vulnerable sites in the body. Once firmly entrenched, immune complexes become sources of constant irritation, inflammation, and, ultimately, dysfunction and destruction of bodily tissue. (Serum sickness and food allergy–induced rheumatoid arthritis are two examples of immune complex–mediated diseases with tissue destruction.)

Since the gut lining never functions perfectly as a barrier, the big difference between a food allergy sufferer and a nonallergic person appears to be the amount of partially digested food that reaches the bloodstream, and how well one's detoxification system clears these allergens from circulation. If large quantities of these foods consistently get in and large quantities of immune complexes are formed, a person will inevitably suffer from delayed food allergy.

The *IgG ELISA laboratory test* (ELISA stands for *E*nzyme *L*inked *I*mmuno *S*orbent *A*ssay) for delayed food allergies involves drawing a single tube of blood and testing it for the presence of IgG antibodies formed against foods in your diet. Depending on the lab doing the testing, this can be done against a hundred or more foods simultaneously. The test's results then are read and recorded by computerized laboratory equipment (not technicians).

If your blood serum contains abnormally high levels of IgG antibody against a particular food, it means you are allergic or sensitized to that food. If there are no abnormally elevated levels of food-specific IgG antibodies in your serum, you do not have a delayed-onset allergy to foods.

The IgG ELISA has other advantages to consider:

- It is not necessary to fast overnight before the blood draw.

- It is relatively painless—one skin prick, one tube of blood, and more than one hundred different foods can be tested.
- It is an automated test that doesn't require people peering through a microscope or individually testing each food. If performed with the appropriate lab quality controls, it is accurate and reproducible.
- The test can be done with serum samples sent through the mail, as long as the sample reaches the licensed reference lab within seventy-two hours of the blood draw.

The IgG ELISA represents a step forward in the field of food allergy testing by addressing the enormously prevalent problem of delayed food allergy head-on; it removes the barriers of inaccuracy and poor reproducibility that continue to plague many competing tests. It is one of the tests I recommend as a screening tool for diagnosing delayed-onset food allergies.

DIAGNOSING CELIAC DISEASE

The Small Bowel Biopsy: Still the Gold Standard

There are one million Americans, both young and old, with celiac disease (CD), but 95 percent of them will go undiagnosed and never be placed on a gluten-free diet. These unsuspecting celiacs will continue to eat wheat and other gluten products. Tragically, many serious, even life-threatening complications, including severe malnutrition and intestinal cancer, may occur later on. It's absolutely imperative, therefore, that celiac disease is diagnosed as early as possible.

Physicians regard the *small-bowel biopsy* as the "gold standard" for the diagnosis of CD. It usually is an outpatient procedure performed by a specialist. A long tube is inserted through the mouth, esophagus, stomach, and finally into the small intestine where several biopsies of mucosa lining are taken. A pathologist looking for the characteristic mucosal lesions of CD studies these small bits of tissue under a microscope. However, as you can imagine, the small-bowel biopsy is an expensive and inconvenient diagnostic tool, and many doctors and their patients are understandably reluctant to engage in the procedure.

This is where modern laboratory science comes into play. Several antibody blood tests currently are being used with great success to help distinguish likely candidates for celiac disease. People with a positive screening now have an excellent reason to have a biopsy performed, and a much higher percentage of biopsies are coming back positive for celiac disease. At the same time, fewer unnecessary and costly biopsies are being done.

SCREENING TESTS FOR CELIAC DISEASE

Anti-gliadin IgG and Anti-gliadin IgA (AGA) Blood Tests

Both the *anti-gliadin IgG test* and the *anti-gliadin IgA test* are used for initial CD screening. The tests are done together in order to maximize the sensitivity of the screening; if you have celiac disease, one or both of the tests will pick it up well over 90 percent of the time. However, a problem may arise even if you don't have celiac disease: One of the tests may still come up positive. Therefore, a more specific screening test needs to be included.

IgA Anti-endomysium Blood Test

That more specific test is the *IgA anti-endomysium test*. It is a more expensive and sophisticated screening test for celiac disease. Due to its expense, it is usually performed only after one or both of the less-expensive AGA tests comes back positive. The anti-endomysium test provides more accurate screening than either or both of the AGA tests—if you have CD, the test comes up positive for IgA antibodies nearly 100 percent of the time. If you don't have celiac disease, unlike the AGA tests, it will come back negative approximately 95 percent of the time.

IgA Anti-transglutaminase (tTG) ELISA

The *IgA anti-transglutaminase (tTG) ELISA* is the newest lab test for celiac disease. This test measures anti-transglutaminase IgA antibodies in human serum. Like the anti-endomysium assay, it is brought into play when either or both of the AGA tests are positive for gliadin antibodies. Studies published in Europe and the United States confirm that the tTG ELISA is equivalent in accuracy to the anti-endomysium test. If positive, it is very likely that you have celiac disease, and without question a follow-up intestinal biopsy is indicated for final confirmation. (My prediction is that the tTG ELISA will soon replace the anti-endomysium assay, and may even replace small-bowel biopsies as the "gold standard.")

Therapies for Food Allergy

FOOD ALLERGEN ELIMINATION AND THE ROTATION DIET

As location is to real estate, strict elimination of allergic foods and rotation of nonallergic foods are to treating food allergy.

Eliminating allergic foods means exactly that. Strict avoidance for three to six months is recommended. This means very careful reading of labels on cans and packages and cautious eating in restaurants. It means a willingness to give up favorite foods and perhaps go through withdrawal or detoxification symptoms the first week of the program. It means feeling deprived and unfilled, not having a "good friend" to temporarily make you feel better. It also means the end of allergic suffering.

Along with eliminating allergic foods and correcting malnutrition and the leaky gut syndrome associated with food allergy, the rotation of nonallergic foods is the single most important way to reverse and prevent recurrence of food allergy.

For the first three months following complete elimination of all food allergens from your diet, carefully rotate and vary all nonallergic foods. None of the nonallergic foods should be eaten more frequently than once every three to four days.

The good news is that after three months of food rotation, you should be able to reintroduce most of the formerly allergic foods back into your daily diet, without allergic symptoms. *Important exceptions to this rule would include gluten in biopsy-proven celiac disease and immediate-onset food allergens that previously have caused anaphylaxis, such as peanuts and shellfish. These foods are permanent, fixed food hypersensitivities, and must be avoided for a lifetime.*

After three months, the principles of food rotation should still guide what and how you eat, although on a much more flexible basis. Nevertheless, the principles of food rotation are the foundation of a lifelong, allergy-free diet.

The following are the five principles of a food allergen–free rotation diet (and why such a program is sensible and effective for everyone):

1. A rotation diet helps prevent the development of allergies and addictions. Food allergies develop for a wide variety of reasons, but a major reason seems to be too frequent and/or too much exposure to a potential food allergen (our Stone Age ancestors, with our same genetic makeup, were forced by seasons and scarcity to rotate and vary their foods).

2. Rotation encourages a more balanced, unprocessed, and varied diet and therefore leads to consuming more

needed nutrients. If you are not going to repeat foods more often than every four days, you will have to get out of your eating rut! Most people's diets consist of no more than ten foods and beverages, ingested almost every day of their lives.

3. Rotation dictates a simple, unrefined, unchemicalized diet. It is almost impossible to continue to eat processed, packaged foods on a rotation diet. Many packaged foods contain not one or two but dozens of food ingredients, which, once eaten, cannot be repeated for seventy-two to ninety-six hours. The same goes for recipes with multiple ingredients and elaborate sauces or gravies.

4. Rotation destresses digestion. A rotation diet—with occasional or frequent involuntary fasting—is what your digestive system genetically was designed to handle. Without overexposure to the same foods, food allergens, "bad" fats and oil, chemicals, additives, and excess refined sugar, your system can strengthen and repair itself. Varied, nutrient- and fiber-rich, nonallergic foods bring about optimal release of gut hormones and digestive juices; help heal and reverse an inflamed, leaky gut lining; improve absorption of nutrients; reduce toxic overload to the liver; and relieve constipation and diarrhea.

5. Rotation leads to weight loss. A rotation diet clears up the allergies that lead to food cravings, overeating, a slowed metabolism, and water retention.

To plan a rotation diet, begin with a list of the foods to which you are not allergic. You may self-test for food allergies, of course, if you have the wisdom of Solomon and patience of Job, or you can make use of the quick and easy laboratory blood tests for delayed food allergy and gluten sensitivity now available (see chapter 5).

The next step is to plan three to four days of menus. Again, the meal plans should avoid all the foods to which you are allergic and should not repeat any one nonallergic food for three or four days. In this planning process, be guided by what you like, the time you have to prepare meals, and what is available at local supermarkets or health food stores. Keep it simple— use just a few foods and ingredients in each meal. If you must avoid protein-rich foods like eggs, beef, and dairy products, make sure you get protein from alternative sources; fresh broiled or baked fish (nonallergic) is a favorite choice of mine.

Here are some additional tips to make your rotation diet a success:

1. Be an alert shopper. Some common allergic foods show up in dozens of popular food items. That is why it is best to eat simple, fresh foods as much as possible.
2. Avoid all alcohol for three months (spirits of any kind are a major cause of a leaky gut).
3. Have a big, fresh, mixed vegetable salad every day (not eating enough fresh vegetables each day is a fundamental cause of allergy). The choice of salad dressing is important. Rotate your oils daily and select only unrefined, cold-pressed oils. My preferences include cold-pressed flaxseed oil, and extra virgin olive oil.
4. Drink eight to twelve 8-ounce glasses of filtered water—without ice—each day. Two or three glasses of water should contain about 4 grams of glutamine each; drink a glass of water thirty minutes before each meal.
5. Try not to eat after 6:00 or 7:00 P.M., and make the last meal of the day a lighter meal.

6. There is no limit, except satisfaction of physiological hunger, on the amount that you eat. Do not count calories, do not remain hungry, and do not starve yourself. Concentrate on good nutrition and your health. If you're overweight, you'll be amazed when your weight begins to plummet—without counting a single calorie.

7. Expect withdrawal or detoxification symptoms when coming off allergic foods. Physiological addiction to food is no different from addiction to alcohol, caffeine, or tobacco. The person who has allergies of a fairly severe nature can expect to go through a withdrawal period lasting three to ten days when he abruptly gives up the allergic foods. The withdrawal symptoms usually reflect an intensification of symptoms you already were having, including headache, fatigue, poor sleep, depression, anxiety, stuffiness, joint aches, digestive upset, and severe food cravings. (One extremely effective treatment to avoid going through severe withdrawals is supplementation with large, therapeutic doses of vitamin C, either orally or intravenously. You begin taking 12 to 20 grams of vitamin C in divided doses the day before elimination of the food and continue for three consecutive days. If diarrhea occurs during this time, reduce dose by 50 percent.)

8. After three months of strict rotation, reintroduce a moderate serving of previously offending foods into your diet, one food at a time every three days. If you're still allergic to certain foods, the three days allow time for delayed food allergic reactions to occur. *(Exceptions to reintroduction include gluten cereals in all celiac*

patients as well as peanuts, shellfish, or any food to which you have a history of anaphylaxis.)

Will I Ever Eat Favorite Foods Again?

Anyone who finds they have food allergies inevitably will ask the question, "Will I ever be able to eat the food(s) again?"

After adhering to the three- to six-month food elimination and rotation program, patients with delayed food allergies eventually are "cleared" of most of their food allergies. If done cautiously, one food at a time, they will be able to reintroduce most of the formerly allergic foods into their diets without allergic symptoms. They should remain allergy-free if they continue to consistently avoid the mistakes and bad dietary choices that led to food allergy in the first place (see chapters 4 and 6).

On the other hand, life is not always fair. People allergic to gluten cereals have a lifelong genetic disease on their hands and need to strictly avoid all sources of gluten the rest of their lives. Other patients may suffer anaphylaxis or severe angioedema from Type 1 immediate-onset reactions to peanuts and shellfish. They will have to carry syringes of adrenaline and antihistamine medication with them at all times. Needless to say, these foods also must be carefully avoided for a lifetime.

PROBIOTICS AND PREBIOTICS

Probiotics

Consider this: There are more individual bacteria organisms normally living in your gastrointestinal tract than there are cells in the human body. In all, there are between 10 and 100 trillion bacteria in each of us, with a total weight of about 5 pounds!

Friendly, health-promoting bacteria are known as *probiotics*. There are some 180 probiotic species now being studied by scientists; these include at least 46 strains of lactobacillus, 9 strains of bifidobacterium, and *Streptococcus thermophilus.*

A 1997 Finnish study found that infants with eczema and cow's milk allergy who were being breast-fed improved significantly when their mothers were given probiotic bacteria supplements. The report concluded by stating, "By alleviating intestinal inflammation, [probiotic supplements] may act as a useful tool in the treatment of food allergy."[21]

Oral probiotic supplementation is rapidly becoming an acceptable, mainstream medical approach for the treatment of food allergy and a wide variety of other health problems. Here's a list of allergy-associated conditions that probiotic supplements help prevent and reverse:

- infant atopic dermatitis
- other food allergies
- abnormally permeable, leaky gut
- intestinal inflammations
- irritable bowel syndrome
- *H. pylori* infections, thought to cause peptic ulcers, gastritis
- virus-, food allergy-, or antibiotic-induced diarrhea, traveler's diarrhea
- restoration of normal levels of friendly bacteria in patients immediately following antibiotic therapy (antibiotics kill off not only infection-causing bacteria but probiotic bacteria as well)
- yeast infections (candidiasis)

Prebiotics

Probiotic bacteria need to eat to survive, and this is where *prebiotics* come into play. Prebiotics are nondigestible, fermentable food ingredients that feed and stimulate friendly bacteria in the intestines. Fermentable fibers increase the densities of beneficial bacteria and stimulate growth and functions of the healthy intestine. Recent findings[22] show that after acute diarrhea, the use of a solution with the fermentable fiber *oligofructose* accelerates recovery of beneficial bacteria, reduces the relative abundance of detrimental, disease-causing bacteria, stimulates intestinal mucosal growth, and enhances digestive and protective immune functions. Prebiotics often are included in probiotic supplements for this reason.

Examples of prebiotics include fructooligosaccharides (FOS), inulin (from fermentable chicory fructan), guar gum, and pectin. (Note that reports of inulin additive sensitivity are on the rise. Caveat emptor!)

My recommendation for all food allergy sufferers: Three times daily, before each meal, take 500 to 1,000 milligrams (10 to 20 billion bacteria) of a natural blend of lactobacilli (e.g., *L. acidophilus, L. plantarum,* and *L. casei*), bifidobacteria (e.g., *B. infantis* and/or *B. faecium*), and *Streptococcus thermophilus*—preferably, take this with FOS, guar, and/or pectin prebiotic.

QUERCETIN BIOFLAVONOID

Food and airborne allergic reactions often involve mast cells. These mast cells are "unstable" in allergy sufferers, and too readily release large quantities of histamine, inflammatory prostaglandins, cytokines, leukotrienes, and other mediators of allergy. In excess, these chemicals cause most of the symptoms of food allergy.

In the earlier years, my approach with food allergy patients was too narrow, limited primarily to identifying and eliminating allergy-causing foods. I would ask my patients to heroically remove numerous favorite foods from their diets for at least three to six months and to rotate nonallergic foods. Most of them would do well for a time, motivated as a result of feeling so much better. Then, slowly, inexorably, most would start slipping back into old habits and old food choices. They found it difficult to stay away from favorite foods in the long term, and found it next to impossible to rotate foods indefinitely. Within six months to a year, old allergy symptoms began returning.

Quercetin is the one daily supplement I have used faithfully over the years, both personally and with those less compliant food allergy patients. I have seen literally hundreds of very symptomatic individuals with multiple food allergies struggling to stay away from favorite allergic foods while rotating their diets. Because of their busy schedules, many eat daily in restaurants and don't have a clue what they are being served. When supplementing their diets with quercetin, however, these same patients find that their allergic symptoms diminish across the board. Sometimes on quercetin alone, allergic foods can be reintroduced without the provocation of symptoms. So, what is quercetin?

Quercetin is a plant bioflavonoid naturally found in wine, but not beer; in tea, but not coffee; in the outer layers of red and yellow onions, but not white onions. Apples, lettuce, chives, berries, cherries, algae, tree bark, and other plants also contain quercetin (notice that many of the sources of quercetin are fruits and vegetables, the very food groups allergy sufferers don't eat enough of).

Quercetin—the most studied, potent, and versatile of all 4,000 or so bioflavonoids—stabilizes mast cells in allergic patients, and is a potent antioxidant and anti-inflammatory agent. For the best effect, quercetin should be taken in combination with vitamin C and a high-potency bromelain.

The effective therapeutic dose for most adults is 250 milligrams of quercetin in combination with approximately 125 milligrams of high-potency bromelain and 250 to 500 milligrams of vitamin C, taken together three to four times a day, thirty minutes before meals. For maintenance (after your allergic symptoms have been brought under good control), reduce the above dose to twice daily, thirty minutes before breakfast and again before dinner.

The growing number of people who choose not to eat lots and lots of fresh fruits and vegetables are undernourished with bioflavonoids, quercetin specifically. If they don't consume more quercetin, they will be more prone to food allergies.

Note: There are other "mast stabilizing" antiallergy herbals that are under investigation. Included among the more promising are *Coleus forskohlii*, extracts from *Picrorhiza kurroa* (Kutki in India), and *Ocimum sanctum* (Tulsi in India).

Glutamine

Glutamine is the most abundant free amino acid in the human body. It is the most important food or fuel for the small intestinal mucosa and the immune system. Like the MSM-derived amino acid known as *cysteine,* glutamine is critical for maintaining optimal levels of the detoxifying antioxidant enzyme glutathione peroxidase. When in ample supply—that is, when you're well and not overly stressed from food allergies, celiac disease, Crohn's disease, ulcerative colitis, HIV or AIDS, chronic inflammations, major injury or trauma from surgery, burns, excessive exercise, or medications—glutamine is able to maintain a healthy intestinal lining and immune system.

If your body is chronically stressed from food allergies or celiac disease and you suffer from the inevitable leaky gut and suppressed immune system that accompanies both, you are suffering from glutamine deficiency. You need glutamine supplementation.

Here are six proven therapeutic benefits of glutamine supplementation:

1. Glutamine increases growth hormone release. Growth hormone also helps to restore and maintain a healthy digestive tract and immune system.
2. Glutamine increases glutathione production in the liver, lymph nodes, and intestinal lining. This helps the body clear food allergen-antibody immune complexes from circulation and prevents an excessive buildup of cell- and tissue-destroying, cancer-causing free radicals.
3. Glutamine helps prevent and reverse the leaky gut seen in food-allergic patients. This includes gluten enteropathy (celiac disease), Crohn's disease, and ulcerative colitis.[23]
4. Glutamine helps prevent intestinal bleeding and ulceration in people taking aspirin and other nonsteroidal anti-inflammatory drugs (NSAIDs) for food allergy–induced chronic pain syndromes such as arthritis, migraines, and fibromyalgia.

5. Glutamine helps prevent or reverse poor nutrient status in food allergy patients with malabsorption.
6. Glutamine helps prevent and heal peptic ulcers, a condition worsened by food allergy.

Recommended dose: 4 grams of glutamine powder mixed in water or diluted fruit juice two to four times a day. (There are powdered glutamine-based formulas with selected antioxidants, quercetin, and standardized anti-inflammatory herbal extracts that I prefer to pure glutamine. However, pure glutamine works well alone.)

Maintenance dose would be 4 grams mixed in tepid water or fruit juice once or twice daily. Do not mix glutamine in ice water or hot water.

MSM: THE NEW KID ON THE BLOCK

Elimination of food allergens, rotation of a wide variety of nonallergic foods, and the daily consumption of five to nine servings of fresh nonallergic fruits and vegetables is the foundation of an effective food allergy program. We have discussed the critical roles that certain nutritional supplements play in helping reverse the underlying causes of food allergy— glutamine, quercetin with vitamin C and bromelain, and probiotics.

MSM (methylsulfonylmethane) is the newest kid on the block. MSM is a nontoxic, natural component of the plants and animals we eat and is normally found in breast milk and in the urine of humans. MSM is an oxidation product of *dimethyl sulfoxide (DMSO)* (but without DMSO's garlic odor) and can be taken orally as a supplement.

At Dr. Stanley Jacob's Oregon Health Sciences University, many clinical benefits have been observed with oral MSM supplementation. The following are some of those benefits:

- Oral MSM has alleviated allergic responses to both food and pollen allergens. The antiallergic property of MSM is reported to be on a par with, or better than, traditional antihistaminic drugs.
- MSM provides relief for migraine headache sufferers.
- Daily MSM supplementation is reported to provide dramatic and long-lasting relief of the pain of rheumatoid arthritis.
- MSM helps prevent and reverse constipation seen in irritable bowel syndrome and in cow's milk–allergic patients.
- MSM helps relieve snoring (a common food allergy symptom).
- Acne, acne rosacea, and other skin problems associated with a leaky gut and food allergy respond favorably to MSM supplementation.
- MSM is particularly helpful in individuals presenting with the pain, stiffness, and swelling of various musculoskeletal disorders.

MSM appears to work in a number of ways to help relieve allergies: MSM binds or coats the lining of the small intestine (this may result in reduction of inflammation and reversal of a leaky gut); it also provides building blocks in the intestinal bacteria's manufacturing of major antiallergy, anti-inflammatory, sulfur-containing amino acids, such as methionine and cysteine.[24] Cysteine then goes on to increase the production of glutathione, the most potent antioxidant, detoxifying enzyme system in the human body. MSM, along with its two sister compounds, DMSO and DMS, is the primary dietary source of sulfur, the fourth most abundant mineral in the human body. Sulfur is part of the chemical makeup of more than 150 compounds in the body (e.g., all the proteins, as well as sulfur-containing amino acids, antibodies, collagen, skin, nails, insulin, growth hormone, and glutathione). Sulfur also makes up cross-linking disulfide bonds—the "railroad ties"—that bind protein filaments together, thereby giving strength and toughness to protein.

I believe sulfur is an essential nutrient, but sulfur deficiency has never been identified, primarily because protein deficiency always coexists. Strict vegetarians (diets without MSM-rich eggs, beef, chicken, fish, or milk products) and people on high-carbohydrate, low-protein diets probably are suffering from suboptimal sulfur intake. Antibiotic overuse also may be contributing to sulfur deficiency by killing off the intestinal bacteria needed to produce essential sulfur-containing amino acids.

Recommended dose: The daily therapeutic dose of MSM ranges from 1,000 milligrams to 6,000 milligrams. It is recommended that an average adult (150 to175 pounds) take 1,500 milligrams two to three times a day, or 3,000 milligrams to 4,500 milligrams total. Like quercetin, MSM has been shown to work better if each dose is taken with 500 to 1,000 milligrams of vitamin C.

Keep in mind that MSM is not like an aspirin or a shot of cortisol. A single, one-time dose of MSM is not effective in ameliorating symptoms. Noticeable anti-inflammatory, anti-allergy, and/or antipain results usually are seen within two to twenty-one days.

MSM supplements have been shown to be as safe as normal drinking water, and MSM is rated as one of the least toxic substances in biology. (A small number of users report experiencing a mild heartburn when they first start taking MSM, but if taken with meals, this shouldn't be a problem. For those of you who end up taking MSM for a longer period of time, it usually doesn't matter whether you take it with food or not.)

OMEGA-3 OILS: THE GOOD FATS

The last three decades have seen a dramatic increase in the prevalence of asthma, eczema, middle ear disease, ADHD, allergic rhinitis, and all other forms of allergy.

This increase in allergy has been paralleled by a decrease in the consumption of dietary oils known as *omega-3 fatty acids.* These oils are abundant in fish, flaxseed, rapeseed, walnuts, and certain bean oils. During the same thirty-year time span, an increase in the consumption of margarine, vegetable oils, and seed oils (omega-6 polyunsaturated fatty acids), and a gradual fall in the consumption of animal fats also has occurred.

Changes in the dietary intake of fats and oils may explain a lot about the increase in food allergies. Too much margarine and vegetable/seed oils and too little fish oil can result in the overproduction of chemical troublemakers—inflammatory prostaglandins and leukotrienes—chemicals that make you more prone to inflammation and allergies.[25]

In a study reported in the 1996 issue of *Medical Journal of Australia,* children who regularly ate fresh, oily fish had a significantly reduced risk of asthma, as well as increased protection from the condition. No other food groups or nutrients were associated with either an increased or reduced risk of current asthma.[26]

We need more (nonallergic) fresh, oily fish and other sources of omega-3 oils in our diet regularly. Two to three 4- to 6-ounce servings of baked or broiled (never fried) salmon, Alaskan halibut, haddock, flounder, cod, red snapper, or trout, accompanied by a bountiful mixed salad covered with cold-pressed flaxseed oil and/or extra virgin olive oil is a meal that makes good food allergy–fighting sense.

VITAMINS AND MINERALS

Vitamin A

Vitamin A is an extremely important antioxidant and immune system–enhancing vitamin. Its functions in the body related to allergy are the following:

- Maintains health of the mucous membranes and skin. Helpful in the prevention and treatment of eczema, psoriasis, and acne.
- Acts as an antioxidant. Controls highly destructive free radicals released during allergic reactions.
- Maintains a healthy thymus gland, the master gland of the immune system.
- Helps prevent excessive inflammatory prostaglandin release during allergic inflammatory reactions.
- With zinc and probiotics, helps in the production of secretory IgA and protective mucus in the digestive tract.
- Offers therapeutic value in the treatment of asthma, inflammatory bowel disease, eczema, rheumatoid arthritis, and other food allergy–related disorders.

With the important exception of premenopausal women, a basic dose of 20,000 IU per day is very safe for most adults, and 10,000 IU really is minimal. *Daily vitamin A supplementation in excess of 5,000 IU is contraindicated in all premenopausal women, as too much vitamin A is associated with birth defects.*

As with all fat-soluble vitamins, there is the possibility of toxicity from overdoses of vitamin A. Individual tolerance levels depend on metabolic demand and general state of health. Most commonly, excess vitamin A is indicated by dry skin, but there also may be irritability, tenderness or aching in the long bones of the body, headaches, cracking at the edges of the lips, hair thinning or hair loss, and abnormal liver function tests. Decreasing or stopping the dosage should relieve the symptoms.

Long-term megadoses of vitamin A—50,000 IU and above—should be taken only under a physician's supervision, and only after tests have been done for liver function, blood levels of vitamin A, and red blood cell sedimentation rates. Follow-up tests should be repeated at four- to six-week intervals. Understanding and recognizing the possible side effects of vitamin A supplementation, however, should not scare you away from including substantial amounts of this vital antiallergy supplement in your program.

Vitamin B$_6$

Vitamin B$_6$, in addition to being a major free radical scavenging antioxidant, plays a big part in the metabolism of essential fatty acids to prostaglandins, and therefore has far-reaching effects on the cardiovascular, digestive, neurological, and immune systems.

Vitamin B$_6$ also has a well-documented connection to learning, behavioral, emotional, and mental processes. It is a critical cofactor in the production of *serotonin,* a neurotransmitter that seems to play an important role in food allergy–induced chronic pain, headaches, and depression.

Here are some allergy-related functions of vitamin B$_6$:

- Improves the production and release of hydrochloric acid (HCl) in the stomach. HCl is often underproduced in the stomachs of food allergy sufferers, probably due to food allergy–induced gut hormone inhibition and malnutrition. B$_6$ works better when used in conjunction with niacin, zinc, and food allergy elimination.
- Helpful in food allergy– or gluten-induced psychological depression and the hyperactivity of ADHD. B$_6$ is essential in the conversion of amino acids into brain neurotransmitters, often found to be at suboptimal levels in these individuals.
- Helpful in the treatment of certain forms of epilepsy and chronic pain syndromes.
- Stimulates the thymus gland, thereby contributing to the formation of antibodies and more optimally functioning immune cells.

Vitamin B$_6$ deficiency is one of the most common nutrient deficiencies in the country. Yet the U.S. RDA (recommended daily allowance) for B$_6$ is pitifully low—just 2 milligrams a day. Some research biochemists believe that a more optimal proper intake should be eight to forty times that. This raises the question of safety: Is vitamin B$_6$ safe for long-term use in large segments of the population, including children?

Studies on children with Down's syndrome and autism, using much higher doses of vitamin B$_6$ than are used for other therapeutic purposes, indicate relative safety. Studies over five to ten years involving adult patients with carpal tunnel syndrome, using 100 to 150 milligrams a day of B_6, have shown minimal or no toxicity. However, women self-treating for PMS who were taking 500 to 5,000 milligrams a day have shown peripheral neuropathy within one to three years.

Recommended dose: Vitamin B_6 is safe at doses of 50 mg to 100 milligrams a day or less in adults; in children, 5 to 50 milligrams a day would be a prudent dose.

Vitamin C: The Natural Antihistamine

Vitamin C seems to be involved in almost all bodily functions. It is needed for the formation of connective tissue, the replacement of old tissue, and the generation of new tissue, making it invaluable for the healing of inflamed tissues and wounds. Healthy teeth and bones depend on its presence for strength and flexibility, as do the walls of capillaries and veins.

The most profound effects, however, are seen in the overall strength of the body's immune system, where vitamin C stimulates certain white blood cells, the *phagocytes,* to seek out and devour food allergens, bacteria, and viruses.

In addition, vitamin C is a natural antihistamine: It enhances the action of the enzyme *histaminase,* which quickly metabolizes histamine. One gram of vitamin C reduces blood histamine by approximately 20 percent, and 2 grams of vitamin C reduces histamine by more than 30 percent, thus reducing the severity of allergic reactions.

Vitamin C also acts as a powerful antioxidant, detoxifying many harmful free-radical substances, both those in the environment and those produced by allergic reactions in the body, and is known to reactivate vitamin E, another powerful antioxidant.

Asthmatics—especially those suffering from exercise-induced asthma—hay fever sufferers, those with food-induced allergic rhinitis, and arthritics all can benefit from the immune support provided by vitamin C.

Recommended dose: 500 milligrams a day is the minimum maintenance dose. The adult therapeutic dose begins at about 2,000 milligrams a day. During severe allergic reactions, 8,000 to 12,000 milligrams daily in divided doses may be indicated.

If you are taking more vitamin C than you need, you may develop a slight diarrhea; this goes away as soon as you cut back on the amount you're taking. Also, calcium oxalate kidney stone formation has been reported as a side effect of large doses of vitamin C, especially in people with previous histories of passing kidney stones.

Individuals with calcium oxalate kidney stones (about 80 percent of all kidney stones) often have deficiencies in magnesium and vitamin B_6. Supplementation with magnesium and B_6 prevents calcium oxalate kidney stone formation.

Magnesium

Magnesium is the second most abundant mineral in the human body. It works closely with calcium, taurine, and vitamin B_6 to regulate the heart, muscles, brain, and immune system. Research has shown that magnesium—often called the "antistress mineral"—has a calming effect, resembling that of a natural sedative.

As a cofactor of essential fatty acid metabolism, magnesium plays a significant role in the prevention and treatment of various forms of allergy, such as premenstrual syndrome, lowered body metabolism, asthma, hyperactivity, autism, and migraine. Intravenous administration of 1 gram of magnesium during an attack reverses migraine headaches in more than 80 percent of the cases. (This is most effective if the migraine sufferer has a low blood level of ionized magnesium at the time of IV therapy.)

Recommended adult dose: 200 milligrams of elemental magnesium as a chelate (e.g., magnesium glycine), one to three times daily.

Zinc

Zinc turns out to be far more influential in the treatment of food allergy than previously realized. It is a vital cofactor of essential fatty acid metabolism. Along with niacin and vitamin B_6, zinc is important for the production of hydrochloric acid in the stomach.

Zinc is a powerful immune-system stimulant that activates the thymus gland, which in turn produces the immune cell-stimulating hormone *thymosin*. Zinc is known to aid in the restoration of the integrity and permeability of the mucosal linings of the air passages and the gastrointestinal tract; in other words, it helps to reverse a leaky gut.

Zinc increases the levels of the protective secretory immunoglobulin A (IgA) in the saliva and in the intestinal tract, and as you will recall, secretory IgA prevents bacteria, yeast, parasites, and food allergens from contacting the lining and passing into the bloodstream. Zinc is also needed for IgG antibody production.

Warning signs of a zinc deficiency include celiac disease, chronic inflammatory skin conditions, injuries or surgical incisions that don't heal, low serum albumin, poor dark-to-light adaptation, poor appetite, anorexia nervosa, retarded growth in a child, abnormal cravings for carbohydrates and sweets, impaired taste or smell, clinical depression, and frequent recurring infections.

Recommended adult dose: Although the RDA for zinc is 15 milligrams per day, doses of 20 to 100 milligrams have had beneficial effects in conditions overrepresented in food allergies and gluten sensitivities, such as acne, dermatitis herpetiformis, eczema, psoriasis, hyperactivity, eating disorders, and learning disabilities. *Daily doses of 50 milligrams or higher should not be continued in excess of three months.* Zinc is known to deplete the body of copper; therefore, it is recommended that 2 to 3 milligrams of copper should be taken daily when you are taking zinc.

BREAST-FEEDING

Protective antibodies and essential nutrients are passed from the mother into her breast milk, protecting the baby against allergies and other illnesses for up to six years or more—if the infant is exclusively breast-fed for at least four to six months. The composition of breast milk changes as the baby grows, adjusting to give all the needed essential nutrients missing in most solid or formula feedings. Breast-feeding improves the population of health-promoting probiotic bacteria in the infant's intestines, and also raises a baby's IQ about five points or more (breast milk is rich in docosahexaenoic acid, a mood-elevating brain food also found in oily fish).

Allergy-related benefits of breast-feeding are well established. They include a reduction in the incidence of the following:

- otitis media
- eczema
- asthma, wheezing (a recent Australian study found that children who were exclusively breast-fed for their first four months or so were 25 percent less likely to be

diagnosed with asthma at six years of age; they also were 41 percent less likely to have wheezed three or more times since they were one year old, and 42 percent less likely to have had their sleep disturbed by wheezing in the past year)
- chronic diarrhea (infectious, allergic, and antibiotic-induced)
- insulin-dependent diabetes (avoidance of early exposure to gluten cereals, soy, and cow's milk in particular)

Breast-feeding benefits the mother, too. She has a lower risk of:

- premenopausal breast cancer (American researchers have found that the risk of breast cancer can be reduced by up to 25 percent by breast-feeding)
- ovarian cancer
- hip fractures later in life

Breast-feeding mothers even seem to get their figures back more quickly than those who bottle-feed their babies! Exclusive breast-feeding—no solid food of any kind—for the first four to six months of the baby's life is strongly recommended.

EXERCISE AND FOOD ALLERGY

And then there is the subject of exercise—or rather, the lack of it. Adequate exercise is more important than ever in our mechanized and polluted world to help prevent allergy and restore optimum health. Improved circulation and oxygenation of tissues, enhanced digestion and elimination, immune system stimulation, accelerated detoxification and neutralization of toxins, and growth hormone release—all of these benefits are provided by prudent, regular exercise, and are badly needed to help us against the allergy epidemic. Conversely, a sedentary life is an allergy-promoting lifestyle.

Recommendations: A mixture of brisk walking, aerobics, weight-lifting, calisthenics, and stretching, forty-five to sixty minutes a day, five days a week.

TREATING AND PREVENTING A LEAKY GUT

Many authorities consider abnormal leakiness or permeability of the small intestinal lining a fundamental cause and complication of food allergy.

This paper-thin intestinal lining is composed of mucosal cells that constantly die and slough off, to be rapidly replaced by new cells every seventy-two hours. Tens of millions of fingerlike microscopic *villi* project from this lining into the *lumen* of the small intestine. It is through these tiny projections that nutrients are absorbed. The intestinal lining also serves as a selective barrier, blocking toxins, poisons, partially digested foods, bacteria, viruses, parasites, and yeast from passage into the bloodstream.

Most of the basic causes of abnormal intestinal permeability or leakiness are known; many are within our control to avoid or reverse. By doing so, we are avoiding and reversing fundamental causes of food allergy.

Here are my recommendations for accomplishing exactly that:

1. Identify and eliminate allergic foods (many times that's all that is required to heal the intestinal lining and reverse a leaky gut).

2. Discontinue all alcoholic beverages while attempting to arrest and reverse food allergy symptoms and disease. *This is extremely important.* Alcohol of any kind increases abnormal permeability and makes allergic reactions to foods more severe and frequent.

3. Decrease or discontinue any unnecessary or excessive use of antibiotics. Overuse and misuse of antibiotics occurs when these drugs are prescribed for *viral* infections of any kind. It follows that antibiotics are useless in the treatment of the common cold, viral sore throat, viral bronchitis, influenza, and viral pneumonia. Antibiotics used to treat most cases of middle ear disease appear to make the recurrence of this disease more frequent and severe. Antibiotics for sinusitis also have proven of no lasting benefit.

4. Supplement with glutamine daily. Glutamine is a conditionally essential amino acid that functions as *the* primary fuel of the small intestinal mucosa; it helps to prevent and reverse a leaky gut, regenerate healthy new villi and mucosal lining cells, improve absorption of nutrients from the diet, increase levels of the detoxifying antioxidant enzyme glutathione, nourish and restore a healthy immune system, and save lives by reducing complications of infections postoperatively in major surgery patients.

5. Supplement with quercetin daily. Quercetin is a potent and versatile plant-derived bioflavonoid (phyto-chemical) that stabilizes mast cells, thereby preventing and reversing a leaky gut. It also functions as an antioxidant, anti-inflammatory, anticancer, and anti-heart disease nutrient. About 80 percent of adult food

allergy sufferers improve when taking therapeutic doses of quercetin with vitamin C and bromelain, thirty minutes before meals three to four times a day (see pages 78–80).

6. Discontinue use or overuse of aspirin and aspirin substitutes (NSAIDs) such as ibuprofen, Advil, Motrin, Clinoril, Naprosin, and Aleve. All contribute to a leaky gut and exacerbate food allergies. Make use of alternative nutritional and herbal anti-inflammatories and analgesics that don't cause a leaky gut, such as *Boswellia serrata*[27], standardized ginger extract, MSM, glucosamine sulfate, and curcuminoids from turmeric.

7. Supplement with Ginkgo biloba (a phosphodiesterase inhibitor)—this blocks the action of phosphodiesterase, thereby inhibiting the release of allergic symptom-causing mediators from mast cells. It also is good for the treatment of allergic asthma.

8. Identify and treat existing parasitical infestations and yeast infections. Untreated parasites and yeast overgrowth in the digestive tract cause chronic leakiness of the gut and contribute to chronic food allergy.

FIVE TO NINE DAILY SERVINGS OF FRUITS AND VEGETABLES

The evidence is quite clear: Allergy-prone individuals who eat the most fruits and vegetables have the fewest allergy problems. Vegetables and fruits are loaded with antiallergy, anti-inflammatory bioflavonoids and other phytochemicals. (For a more detailed discussion, see chapter 4, pages 54–55.)

Summary

An epidemic of allergy is accompanying us into the twenty-first century, with delayed-onset food allergies and gluten sensitivity leading the way.

As this book explains, medicine and laboratory science have progressed a long way in understanding food allergy and celiac disease. We know much more about the origins of these conditions and the many different illnesses in which food allergy and celiac disease show themselves. Long-awaited advancements in laboratory testing now allow us to diagnose immediate and delayed food allergy, gluten sensitivity, and celiac disease more accurately than ever before.

With a deeper, broader understanding of food allergy, for the first time we can confidently treat the many causes of food allergy as well as its symptoms—precisely the means by which epidemics of human disease of any kind have been and will continue to be conquered.

Permanent relief from food allergy is not a false promise or a pipe dream. It's a reality and within your reach right now. Go for it!

Notes

1. M. Fuchs, [Food allergies] "D¨etsk'e odd¨elen'i Fakultn'i nemocnice Bulovka," *Praha. Cas Lek Cesk* 137, no. 18 (21 September 1998): 547–51.

2. S. J. Galli, The Paul Kallos Memorial Lecture, "The Mast Cell: A Versatile Effector Cell for a Challenging World," *International Archives of Allergy and Immunology* 113, nos. 1–3 (May 1997): 14–22.

3. R. Malaviya and S. N. Abraham, "Clinical Implications of Mast Cell-Bacteria Interaction," *Journal of Molecular Medicine* 76, no. 9 (August 1998): 617–23.

4. T. Yameda et al., "Alternate Occurrence of Allergic Disease and an Unusual Form of Interstitial Cystitis," *International Journal of Urology* 5, no. 4 (July 1998): 329–35, discussion 335–36.

5. D. R. Altman and L. T. Chiaramonte, "Public Perception of Food Allergy," *Journal of Allergy and Clinical Immunology* 97, no. 6 (June 1996): 1247–51.

6. B. Bellioni et al., "Allergenicity of Goat's Milk in Children with Cow's Milk Allergy," *Journal of Allergy and Clinical Immunology* 103, no. 6 (June 1999): 1191–94; A. W. Burks et al., "Prospective Oral Food Challenge Study of Two Soybean Protein Isolates in Patients with Possible Milk or Soy Protein Enterocolitis," *Pediatric Allergy & Immunology* 5, no. 1 (February 1994): 40–45; R. K. Chandra, "Five-Year Follow-Up of High-Risk Infants with Family History of Allergy Who Were Exclusively Breast-Fed or Fed Partial Whey Hydrolysate, Soy, and Conventional Cow's Milk Formulas," *Journal of Pediatric Gastroenterology & Nutrition* 24, no. 4 (April 1997): 380–88; D. J. Hill et al., "Challenge Confirmation of Late-Onset Reactions to Extensively Hydrolyzed Formulas in Infants with Multiple Food Protein Intolerance," *Journal of Allergy and Clinical Immunology* 96, no. 3 (September 1995): 386–94; A. Høst et al., "The Natural History of Cow's Milk Protein Allergy/Intolerance," *European Journal of Clinical Nutrition* 49, supp. 1 (September 1995): S13–18; G. Iacono et al., "Intolerance of Cow's Milk and Chronic Constipation in Children," *The New England Journal of Medicine* 339, no. 16 (October 1998): 1100–04; J. Maldonado et al., "Special Formulas in Infant Nutrition: A Review," *Early Human Development* 53, supp. (December 1998): S23–32; A. Paganus et al., "Follow-Up of Nutritional Status and Dietary Survey in Children with Cow's Milk Allergy," *Acta Pediatrica* 81, nos. 6–7 (June 1992): 518–21; P. Spuergin et al., "Allergenicity of Alpha-Caseins from Cow, Sheep, and Goat," *Allergy* (March 1997); B. Weisselberg et al., "A Lamb-Meat-Based Formula for Infants Allergic to Casein Hydrolysate Formulas," *Clinical Pediatrics* (Phila) 35, no. 10 (October 1996): 491–95; S. J. Werfel et al., "Clinical Reactivity to Beef in Children Allergic to Cow's Milk,"

Journal of Allergy and Clinical Immunology 99, no. 3 (March 1997): 293–300; R. S. Zeiger et al., "Soy Allergy in Infants and Children with IgE-Associated Cow's Milk Allergy," *Journal of Pediatrics* 134, no. 5 (May 1999): 614–22.

7. Spuergin et al., "Allergenicity of Alpha-Caseins."

8. R. M. Rosenfeld, "What to Expect from Medical Treatment of Otitis Media," *Pediatric Infectious Disease Journal* 14 (1995): 731–38; P. Van den Broek et al., letter to the editor, *Lancet* 348 (1996): 1517; R. L. Williams et al., "Use of Antibiotics in Preventing Recurrent Acute Otitis Media and in Treating Otitis Media with Effusion," *Journal of the American Medical Association* 270 (1993): 1344–51.

9. A. Soutar, "Bronchial Reactivity and Dietary Antioxidants," *Thorax* 52, no. 2 (February 1997): 166–70.

10. J. Egger et al., "Oligoantigenic Treatment of [Sixty-Three] Children with Epilepsy and Migraine," *Journal of Pediatrics* 114 (1989): 51–58.

11. C. P. Sandiford et al., "Identification of the Major Water/Salt Insoluble Wheat Proteins Involved in Cereal Hypersensitivity," *Clinical Experimental Allergy* 27, no. 10 (1997): 1120–29.

12. W. T. Cooke and G. K. T. Holmes, *Coeliac Disease* (London: Churchill Livingstone, 1984), 81–105.

13. G. Meloni et al., "Subclinical Coeliac Disease in School Children from Northern Sardinia," *Lancet* 353 (2 January 1999): 37.

14. R. Hoggan, "Considering Wheat, Rye, and Barley Proteins as Aids to Carcinogens," *Medical Hypotheses* 49, no. 3 (September 1997): 285–88.

15. G. Dotevall et al., "Symptoms in Irritable Bowel Syndrome," *Scandinavian Journal of Gastroenterology* 79, supp. (1982): 16–19.

16. R. D. Wagner et al., "Biotherapeutic Effects of Probiotic Bacteria on Candidiasis in Immunodeficient Mice," *Infection & Immunology* 65, no. 10 (October 1997): 4165–72.

17. Hisako Yasui et al., "Protection Against Influenza Virus Infection of Mice Fed Bifidobacterium Breve YIT4064," *Clinical and Diagnostic Laboratory Immunology* 6, no. 2 (March 1999): 186–92.

18. M. Kulig et al., "Long-Lasting Sensitization to Food During the First Two Years Precedes Allergic Airway Disease," The MAS Study Group, Germany, *Pediatric Allergy & Immunology* 9, no. 2 (May 1998): 61–67.

19. C. Svanes, *Journal of Allergy and Clinical Immunology* 103 (1999): 415–20.

20. S. M. Tariq et al., "The Prevalence of and Risk Factors for Atopy in Early Childhood: A Whole Population Birth Cohort Study," *Journal of Allergy and Clinical Immunology* 101, no. 5 (May 1998): 587–93.

21. H. Majamaa and E. Isolauri, "Probiotics: A Novel Approach in the Management of Food Allergy," *Journal of Allergy and Clinical Immunology* 99, no. 2 (February 1997): 179–85.

22. R. K. Buddington and E. Weiher, Department of Biological Sciences, Mississippi State University, "The Application of Ecological Principles and Fermentable Fibers to Manage the Gastrointestinal Tract Ecosystem," *Journal of Nutrition* 129, supp. 7 (July 1999): S1446–50.

23. Ibid.

24. V. L. Richmond, "Incorporation of Methylsulfonylmethane Sulfur into Guinea Pig Serum Proteins," *Life Sciences* 39, no. 3 (July 1986): 263–68.

25. P. Lack et al., *Journal of Allergy and Clinical Immunology* 103 (1999): 351–52.

26. L. Hodge et al., "Consumption of Oily Fish and Childhood Asthma," *Medical Journal of Australia* 164, no. 3 (February 1996): 137–40.

27. *Planta Medica* 55 (1989): 235–42; *Planta Medica* 57, no. 3 (1991): 203–07.

Bibliography

Altman, D. R., and L. T. Chiaramonte. "Public Perception of Food Allergy." *Journal of Allergy and Clinical Immunology* 97, no. 6 (June 1996): 1247–51.

Bellioni, B., et al. "Allergenicity of Goat's Milk in Children with Cow's Milk Allergy." *Journal of Allergy and Clinical Immunology* 103, no. 6 (June 1999): 1191–94.

Buddington, R. K., and E. Weiher, Department of Biological Sciences, Mississippi State University. "The Application of Ecological Principles and Fermentable Fibers to Manage the Gastrointestinal Tract Ecosystem." *Journal of Nutrition* 129, supp. 7 (July 1999): S1446–50.

Burks, A. W., et al. "Prospective Oral Food Challenge Study of Two Soybean Protein Isolates in Patients with Possible Milk or Soy

Protein Enterocolitis." *Pediatric Allergy & Immunology* 5, no. 1 (February 1994): 40–45.

Chandra, R. K. "Five-Year Follow-Up of High-Risk Infants with Family History of Allergy Who Were Exclusively Breast-Fed or Fed Partial Whey Hydrolysate, Soy, and Conventional Cow's Milk Formulas." *Journal of Pediatric Gastroenterology & Nutrition* 24, no. 4 (April 1997): 380–88.

Cooke, W. T., and G. K. T. Holmes. *Coeliac Disease.* London: Churchill Livingstone, 1984.

Dotevall, G., et al. "Symptoms in Irritable Bowel Syndrome." *Scandinavian Journal of Gastroenterology* 79, supp. (1982): 16–19.

Egger, J., et al., "Oligoantigenic Treatment of [Sixty-Three] Children with Epilepsy and Migraine." *Journal of Pediatrics* 114 (1989): 51–58.

Fuchs, M. [Food allergies] "D¨etsk'e odd¨elen'i Fakultn'i nemocnice Bulovka." *Praha. Cas Lek Cesk* 137, no. 18 (21 September 1998): 547–51.

Galli, S. J. The Paul Kallos Memorial Lecture. The Mast Cell: A Versatile Effector Cell for a Challenging World. *International Archives of Allergy and Immunology* 113, nos. 1–3 (May 1997): 14–22.

Hanson, L. A. "Breastfeeding Provides Passive and Likely Long-Lasting Immunity." *Annals of Allergy, Asthma & Immunology* 81, no. 6 (December 1998): 523–33, 537.

Hill, D. J., et al. "Challenge Confirmation of Late-Onset Reactions to Extensively Hydrolyzed Formulas in Infants with Multiple Food Protein Intolerance." *Journal of Allergy and Clinical Immunology* 96, no. 3 (September 1995): 386–94.

Hodge, L., et al. "Consumption of Oily Fish and Childhood Asthma." *Medical Journal of Australia* 164, no. 3 (February 1996): 137–40.

Hoggan, R. "Considering Wheat, Rye, and Barley Proteins as Aids to Carcinogens." *Medical Hypotheses* 49, no. 3 (September 1997): 285–88.

Høst, A., et al. "The Natural History of Cow's Milk Protein Allergy/Intolerance." *European Journal of Clinical Nutrition* 49, supp. 1 (September 1995): S13–18.

Iacono, G., et al. "Intolerance of Cow's Milk and Chronic Constipation in Children." *The New England Journal of Medicine* 339, no. 16 (October 1998): 1100–04.

Kulig, M., et al. "Long-Lasting Sensitization to Food During the First Two Years Precedes Allergic Airway Disease." The MAS Study Group, Germany, *Pediatric Allergy & Immunology* 9, no. 2 (May 1998): 61–67.

Lack, P., et al. *Journal of Allergy and Clinical Immunology* 103 (1999): 351–52.

Li, J., et al. "Glutamine Prevents Parenteral Nutrition-Induced Increases in Intestinal Permeability." *Journal of Parenteral and Enteral Nutrition* 18 (1994): 3030–307.

Majamaa, H., and E. Isolauri. "Probiotics: A Novel Approach in the Management of Food Allergy." *Journal of Allergy and Clinical Immunology* 99, no. 2 (February 1997): 179–85.

Malavia, R., and S. N. Abraham. "Clinical Implications of Mast Cell-Bacteria Interaction." *Journal of Molecular Medicine* 76, no. 9 (August 1998): 617–23.

Maldonado, J., et al. "Special Formulas in Infant Nutrition: A Review." *Early Human Development* 53, supp. (December 1998): S23–32.

Meloni, G., et al. "Subclinical Coeliac Disease in School Children from Northern Sardinia." *Lancet* 353 (2 January 1999): 37.

Paganus, A., et al. "Follow-Up of Nutritional Status and Dietary Survey in Children with Cow's Milk Allergy." *Acta Pediatrica* 81, nos. 6–7 (June 1992): 518–21.

Planta Medica 55 (1989): 235–42.

Planta Medica 57, no. 3 (1991): 203–07.

Richmond, V. L. "Incorporation of Methylsulfonylmethane Sulfur into Guinea Pig Serum Proteins." *Life Sciences* 39, no. 3 (July 1986): 263–68.

Rosenfeld, R. M. "What to Expect from Medical Treatment of Otitis Media." *Pediatric Infectious Disease Journal* 14 (1995): 731–38.

Sandiford, C. P., et al. "Identification of the Major Water/Salt Insoluble Wheat Proteins Involved in Cereal Hypersensitivity." *Clinical Experimental Allergy* 27, no. 10 (1997): 1120–29.

Soutar, A. "Bronchial Reactivity and Dietary Antioxidants." *Thorax* 52, no. 2 (February 1997): 166–70.

Spuergin, P., et al. "Allergenicity of Alpha-Caseins from Cow, Sheep, and Goat." *Allergy* (March 1997).

Svanes, C. *Journal of Allergy and Clinical Immunology* 103 (1999): 415–20.

Tariq, S. M., et al. "The Prevalence of and Risk Factors for Atopy in Early Childhood: A Whole Population Birth Cohort Study." *Journal of Allergy and Clinical Immunology* 101, no. 5 (May 1998): 587–93.

Van den Broek, P., et al. Letter to the editor. *Lancet* 348 (1996): 1517.

Wagner, R. D., et al. "Biotherapeutic Effects of Probiotic Bacteria on Candidiasis in Immunodeficient Mice." *Infection & Immunology* 65, no. 10 (October 1997): 4165–72.

Weisselberg, B., et al. "A Lamb-Meat-Based Formula for Infants Allergic to Casein Hydrolysate Formulas." *Clinical Pediatrics* (Phila.) 35, no. 10 (October 1996): 491–95.

Werfel, S. J., et al. "Clinical Reactivity to Beef in Children Allergic to Cow's Milk." *Journal of Allergy and Clinical Immunology* 99, no. 3 (March 1997): 293–300.

Williams, R. L., et al. "Use of Antibiotics in Preventing Recurrent Acute Otitis Media and in Treating Otitis Media with Effusion." *Journal of the American Medical Association* 270 (1993): 1344–51.

Yameda, T., et al. "Alternate Occurrence of Allergic Disease and an Unusual Form of Interstitial Cystitis." *International Journal of Urology* 5, no. 4 (July 1998): 329–35, discussion 335–36.

Yasui, Hisako, et al. "Protection Against Influenza Virus Infection of Mice Fed Bifidobacterium Breve YIT4064." *Clinical and Diagnostic Laboratory Immunology* 6, no. 2 (March 1999): 186–92.

Zeiger, R. S., et al. "Soy Allergy in Infants and Children with IgE-Associated Cow's Milk Allergy." *Journal of Pediatrics* 134, no. 5 (May 1999): 614–22.

Index